A HOME BY THE SEA

A HOME BY THE SEA

LIZ SEYMOUR

FRIEDMAN/FAIRFAX
PUBLISHERS

A FRIEDMAN/FAIRFAX BOOK
Please visit our website: www.metrobooks.com

Library of Congress Cataloging-in-Publication Data

Seymour, Liz.
    A home by the sea / Liz Seymour.
      p.cm.
    Includes index.
    ISBN 1-56799-800-3 (alk. paper)
      1. Seaside architecture—United States.   2. Vacation homes—United States.
    3. Interior decoration—United States.   4. Lifestyles—United States.   I. Title.

NA7575 .S49 2000
728'37'097309146—dc21
                                                                                    00-039410

Editor: Susan Lauzau
Art Director: Jeff Batzli
Design: Lindgren/Fuller Design
Photography Editor: Kate Perry
Production Manager: Rosy Ngo

Color separations by Dai Nippon
Printed in Hong Kong Dai Nippon Printing Company Limited

1 3 5 7 9 10 8 6 4 2

Distributed by Sterling Publishing Company, Inc.
387 Park Avenue South
New York, NY 10016
Distributed in Canada by Sterling Publishing
Canadian Manda Group
One Atlantic Avenue, Suite 105
Toronto, Ontario, Canada M6K 3E7
Distributed in Australia by
Capricorn Link (Australia) Pty Ltd.
P.O. Box 6651
Baulkham Hills, Business Centre, NSW 2153, Australia

A special thanks to Jason Miller, who supplied additional material.
Thank you also to Kathy Y. Croy of Erickson Interiors and Barbara
McQueen of Barbara McQueen Interior Design, who offered many
of the creative ideas that appear in sidebars.

CONTENTS

It's an annual migration, as dependable and—with bright beach towels, umbrellas, and bathing suits—nearly as colorful as the swallows that return every year to San Juan Capistrano, California, or the monarch butterflies that flutter through Cape May, New Jersey, on their way south. The floodgates open in early June as soon as school doors close. Traveling by car, by boat, and even by bicycle, suitcases packed for a week or, if they are lucky, for a whole glorious summer, families head back to the sea, reclaiming their idyllic patch of coastline.

A family house by the sea is a fixed point in a transient universe; the kind of place in which children grow up knowing every nook and cranny by heart. Surrounded by uncles and aunts, grandparents and cousins, children settle quickly into familiar routines. They tumble from the car as soon as it stops in the driveway. Quickly, they run inside to reacquaint themselves with the smells and textures of the old place, opening windows and doors to banish winter dust and spring cobwebs.

Behind them, moving at a more leisurely pace, adults walk through the house taking inventory of what has survived the

A rambling landscape brushes the edges of Great Island in Cape Cod Bay, Massachusetts. Wild grasses pin the wind-driven sand to swells in the land; the persistent stroke of the tides smooths away the rest.

off-season and what needs repair. Is there a loose railing on the deck, or perhaps water stains on the carpet where the lash of a winter storm crept in around the door? The jobs are not burdensome, representing no more than a pleasant occasional occupation for the weeks ahead, along with scraping and painting the boats, making pickles and homemade jam from the bounty of local farm stands, and teaching the youngest children to swim in the surf.

The house's eccentricities are as familiar as those of an old friend. Some doors stick while others never quite close all the way. Water pipes thump and clank in the night. On chilly nights, the seldom-used antique heating system kicks on, startling light sleepers wide awake. The quirks are also decorative and personal. No rooms are off limits. Everything is washable or so comfortably worn that it is beyond worry. There are timeless plump sofas covered in faded chintz, deep chairs for reading, cushioned alcoves and window seats dimpled with the permanent imprint left by generations of sitters. A jigsaw puzzle is always in progress on a card table, but never finished since some long-ago dog chewed up the last pieces. Rocking chairs creak. The yellowed guest book has been filled over the decades with the effusive thank yous of visitors, enabling one to trace a single biography from looping childish letters to sure

adult handwriting. Some rooms bear names confusing to newcomers—"the old dining room," "Peter's room," "the ivy porch."

Weather and tides are the most important news of the day. In the morning, screen doors bang and the children are off cycling along the shore road on battered communal bicycles. An entire day can be spent in the delightful, serious business of gathering ingredients for the family dinner. Vegetables are culled from the garden or carefully selected at a nearby vegetable stand. A trip down to the pier supplies the catch of the day. A stop at the village bakery yields oven-fresh bread. At day's end, a row of sun-bleached sneakers sits drying on the porch near a pile of bright orange life jackets.

But we are not the first generations to discover the pleasures of the seaside. For centuries, if not millennia, people have been drawn to the abundance of sun and sand and the breezy comfort of life at the water's edge. Wherever beaches have formed, people have followed—houses by the sea have a long and distinguished pedigree. Ancient Romans relaxed in seaside villas ornamented with fabulous mosaics and sculptures. Nineteenth-century Britons praised the sea's health-giving properties and turned towns like Brighton and Torquay into busy resorts. French families trooped to Trouville, Dieppe, and Cannes; wealthy émigrés from Russia, London, and Paris built seaside homes among the vineyards and olive orchards of the French Riviera.

In the mid-nineteenth century, the North American seaside resort was born. Cape May, among the most venerable of coastal resort towns, sits at the southern tip of New Jersey, where the Delaware Bay meets the Atlantic Ocean. As travel became easier, visitors began arriving in this pretty resort from Philadelphia, New York, and Washington, D.C. After a devastating fire in 1878, the town was rebuilt with grand, extravagant houses in the popular Victorian styles—Queen Anne, Gothic Revival, and French Second Empire.

Today, the historic town constitutes the United States' largest collection of Victorian houses, with more than six hundred pre-twentieth-century gingerbread houses lined up along the shady, gas-lit streets. Since 1970, when the whole town was designated a landmark, homeowners have carefully and lovingly restored the houses to their original splendor, complete with lively three-color paint schemes.

By the turn of the century, beach communities had sprung up all along the northeastern Atlantic coast, from Cape Breton, Novia Scotia, to Bar Harbor, Maine, south to the Chesapeake Bay. Sleepy fishing villages found themselves reborn, as wealthy city dwellers restored colonial cottages and built rambling new vacation houses. As trains, steamers, and, later, automobiles put more and more of the coast within reach, inland dwellers fell thoroughly and completely in love with the sea. It's no surprise, then, that today seaside houses dot virtually every stretch of the North American coast.

Though houses along various shorelines and in different beach communities may be vastly different, they share the magic that occurs at the tide line. Stand for a moment with your toes in the water, tasting the salt air and letting your eyes slowly adjust to the long view. As your gaze drifts along the curve of the shore, take in the sparkle of sun on the water, the flash of a gull's wing, the slant of light on the rocks. Maybe the tide is going out, or perhaps it's coming in. Regardless, the scene is ever-changing. And so—and this is the secret of every house by the sea—are we.

CHAPTER ONE

A HOUSE FOR EVERY SHORE

Every stretch of coast has its own character, and even the sand is subtly different. In New England the pale, sugary beaches are made mostly of quartz, but become mixed with garnet and tourmaline as one travels south to Long Island. The sand of the New Jersey shore is smoky quartz; pulverized shells enter the mix in North Carolina. Along the upper Florida coast, the beach is made up of rock fragments washed down eons ago from the highlands of Georgian and South Carolina and mixed further south with sparkling crystals of zircon. Around the Florida Keys, the rosy sand is almost all shell and coral. The green beaches of Oregon and Washington State are made of weathered basalt, and California's coast meets the sea at beautiful agate beaches.

And like the differing character of the sand, each stretch of coastline harbors varying types of houses, all adapted to their singular settings and outfitted for the vagaries of that shoreline's weather. In the following pages we'll take a look at the houses that have evolved in different coastal environments, from sandy beaches to rocky shores to soaring cliff tops.

Though the house appears stranded, it is connected to the mainland by a long spit along which runs a road. Still, the illusion of solitude is complete. When night falls here, it swallows all.

RIGHT: *This house, anchored on thick beams set deeply into the sand, is designed to rise high above storm-driven floods. Newly constructed, the house borrows from a variety of architectural traditions: its metal roof points toward a Low Country vernacular, while the stacked porches recall houses in old Memphis neighborhoods.*

OPPOSITE: *A porch transitions gracefully into a boardwalk that beckons family and guests down to the turquoise sea. Crisp white railings and subtle gingerbread trim make supremely elegant the passage from house to outdoor room to pristine beach.*

AT WATER'S EDGE

A home at the water's edge places the pleasures of the beach at your doorstep. And because the beach is the focus of attention, many of these houses are devoid of fussy ornamentation. With architectural inessentials stripped away, we are made more aware of the house's powerful character: the silhouette of the roof line, the silvery sheen of weathered shingles, the reflection of the evening sky along a row of windows, the gentle calligraphy of a storm fence angling away from one corner of the house and disappearing across the dunes.

More than any other kind of house, a seaside dwelling must respect its setting. It must be sited well above the high-water mark, a rule dictated both by common sense and by building codes (90 percent of storm damage occurs within 600 feet [183m] of the water line). Everything from roof line to foundation is designed with the weather in mind. A roof that is too steep will be battered by storm winds, while one that is too shallow can be lifted off entirely (research shows that the best pitch for a beach house roof is between five and six inches [12–15cm] for every foot [30cm]). Building materials are chosen for their ability to stand up to water, salt, and sun, and windows are placed to take in the view. Like the dunes, a well-built beach house is shaped by the elements, simple by necessity and beautiful in its graceful concessions to the sea.

Often, a particular coastline has a say in a beach house's design. On the barrier islands of the southern Atlantic coast, for example, where the transient shoreline changes from year to year, and even from storm to storm, houses rest on stilts that are anchored deep in the ground. The soft sand and tidewater marshes that mark the coast from the Chesapeake peninsula to the Florida Keys are more amenable to pilings than to brick foundations. Some of the most memorable stilt-style beach houses don't sit at the water's edge, but actually stand in the water.

Houses elevated on stilts are sometimes designed as "upside-down" houses—the usual order of floors is reversed to take advantage of lovely views. Thus, the bottom level contains a carport; storage lockers for sports equipment; space for heating, air-conditioning, and other mechanical systems; and a couple of outdoor showers for washing off the day's accumulation of sand. The next level up accommodates bedrooms and baths—the areas to which occupants retreat at night, but in which they spend little time during the day. It is the third floor that is the crowning jewel of the house. Graced by breathtaking panoramic views, this is the level where the main gathering areas—living room, dining room, and kitchen—are situated. If zoning regulations allow, a master suite is sometimes tucked into the very top of the structure, usually in attic space beneath the roof.

In sultry Southern towns such as Beaufort, South Carolina, or Pass Christian, Mississippi, historic styles owe as much to the climate as they do to prevailing architectural fashion. In towns such as these, wide piazzas are more than decorative—before air conditioning, they were the places where families gathered in the jasmine-scented twilight to enjoy the evening sea breezes. The deep overhangs, high ceilings, and tall sash windows—sometimes triple-hung so they could be opened from the top as well as the bottom—all evolved to handle the heat.

The marshes, estuaries, and sea islands of the South Carolina and Georgia coasts are dotted with old houses characterized by standing-seam metal roofs, often painted a cheerful red. Their foundations are made of "tabby," a local cementlike material made of crushed oyster shells. In Louisiana, French culture and language survived long after the region became part of the United States. It thus comes as no surprise that French architectural traditions also survived and were adapted to the climate. A prime example is the house plan that has become known as the Cajun Cottage. Generously proportioned, but often only one room deep to allow for cross-ventilation, and raised on tall foundations to keep the house safe from flooding, the Cajun Cottage is wrapped in a double-height gallery. Besides providing outdoor living space, the gallery shades the interior from the intense sun and allows windows to be left open for cooling during the almost daily rain showers.

The traditional deep-galleried southern coastal house is just as appropriate today as it was a hundred years ago. A pier foundation elevates the house above the water line, leaving space beneath the first floor for storage. With the functional living space extended by deeply shaded porches and balconies, the interior can be open, with public spaces flowing comfortably into one another.

An unadorned Cape Cod–style house eyes a quiet sea. One of the most uncomplicated architectural styles, the Cape Cod is the epitome of graceful simplicity.

In New England and on Long Island, where the shoreline is relatively stable and hurricanes are infrequent, beach houses may sit on conventional foundations. This is where the ubiquitous Cape Cod–style house, with its simple gable and shed roof, is truly at home. This charming architectural form speaks to so many beachgoers that a large number of new houses built in the Northeast borrow the traditional gray shingles and white trim, double-hung windows, old-fashioned gambrel roofs, and wide, inviting porches.

Los Angeles–area beach houses, on the other hand, often take their cues not from fisherman's shacks and sea captain's houses, but from the designs of such twentieth-century architects as Rudolph Schindler and Richard Neutra. In 1926, the forward-thinking Schindler forever shook up the conventions of beach-house design by building a severely geometrical concrete house in Newport Beach, California. Two decades later, Neutra built a streamlined house with a long ribbon of windows on the beach at Santa Monica for a movie-mogul client. The spare modernist vocabulary of these two architects works well in an area where there is little room for structural ramblings. Instead, flights of fancy are reserved for the interior, which is often rich with mahogany and stainless steel, fine furniture and fine art.

The large population of Southern California presents design challenges that are as powerful as those posed by the landscape. In many beach communities, oceanfront property is so precious that the houses are slotted tightly into narrow lots with sometimes no more than ten feet (3m) between them. The tunnellike homes have thick concrete and structural steel walls—practical in an earthquake zone—that muffle the sound of traffic on the nearby Pacific Coast Highway. Because the structures are sited so close together, they have the potential to be somewhat dark inside. Often, these close quarters mean that direct light is able to enter only through the front windows facing the beach. To compensate, architects have devised a variety of ingenious ways to introduce more natural light, including the use of exterior walls of glass block or frosted glass. Inside the home, three-quarter-height walls are sometimes used to allow light to flow from one room to the next. A similar effect can be achieved by incorporating interior walls—and even ceilings—made of translucent fiberglass. Another light-harvesting strategy dates back to the Romans: the inclusion of an interior atrium illuminated by a skylight.

Farther up the California coast at windy Stinson Beach, twenty miles (32km) north of San Francisco, the look of the houses is vastly different. Homes are designed with sheltered courtyards and windbreaks that give them a distinctive, almost Asian style. In the highly corrosive salt air, siding and decks are held together with stainless steel nails, and steel door frames and railings are protected with a tough, baked-on enamel finish. Some houses are built on a base of concrete block, which is not only sturdy but heats up gently in the afternoon sun and radiates warmth well into the

ABOVE: *This villa borrows from the luxurious architectural styles and sunwashed colors of the French Riviera to deliver an exotic flavor. Deep porches outfitted with ceiling fans help to keep both indoor and outdoor temperatures bearable.*

evening. The lessons of Stinson Beach have been applied to many windy coastal locations.

With the varying architectural styles come different tones and personas. Beach houses can be modest, like a simple shingled saltbox, or grand, like architect Addison Mizner's extravagant 1920s Spanish-style Palm Beach mansions, their green lawns protected from a narrow beach behind a concrete seawall. They can ramble with porches and balconies, like the gray shingled family compounds on tiny Shelter Island—a mere ferry ride away from Long Island's fashionable Hamptons—or they can take the form of severely modern cubes, like the mansions of movie stars in Malibu.

Some beach houses even exude a jazzy air. The ice cream–colored Art Deco fantasies of Miami's South Beach certainly fall into this category. Following its initial heyday, which lasted from the 1930s to the 1950s, South Beach was neglected for a good period of time. But in the 1970s, the area's Art Deco confections were rediscovered by a new generation of architects and art historians. Since then, a continuing preservation effort has seen the restoration of more than eight hundred buildings, and the area currently attracts an international cadre of celebrities, models, and photographers, all eager to see and be seen.

ROCKY SHORES

On the Atlantic Coast, the beckoning arm of Cape Cod divides the coast, with rugged shore to the north and gentle beach to the south. North of Cape Cod, the advance of glaciers bent the earth's crust so precipitously that the sea rushed in, turning sand dunes into off-shore shoals, and transforming hills, valleys, and ridges into a new seacoast. This glacial movement also sculpted the soft stone of Cape Breton Island and New Brunswick into raw, jagged silhouettes. Along the Pacific Coast, enormous and dynamic geological plates are still sliding past each other, creating a dramatic, craggy coastline.

East or West, it is impossible to ignore nature's power on these rocky shores. It is here that the sea surges in booming waves across masses of boulders. The strongest tides in the world are found at the Bay of Fundy, which separates New Brunswick from Nova Scotia. Indeed, it can take only a few hours for the water to rise 20 feet (6m) or more. On the opposite side of the continent, above the turbulent shores of California's Monterey Peninsula, nature's incredible strength is evident in the trees, which were shaped and twisted into fantastic forms by the wind. On the coast of Oregon, sea lions sun themselves on sharp boulders that have

LEFT: *An inviting gazebo overlooks a watery panorama. The shake roof, rough-sawn support timbers, and railing details echo the log architecture of the neighboring house.*

BELOW: *Even with its generous size, this log home, with its native materials and honest construction, immediately evokes a sense of warmth and comfort. Forest green trim and a cedar shake roof complete the link with the surrounding woods. Steep rooflines help to shed snow during winter storms, an important feature in a northerly locale.*

OPPOSITE: *A rambling, split-rail fence prevents anyone craning for a view from tumbling into the Pacific. Hewn from cedar, this rustic fence is made from one of the few woods that can withstand the salt air that roars up the cliff face.*

claimed hundreds of shipwrecks. And all along the northern Pacific coast, the ocean ceaselessly carves rock outcroppings into breathtaking arches and precariously balanced pillars.

When you turn inland from a rocky shoreline, the view often consists of scrubby stands of bayberry and juniper, or, on the Pacific coast, clumps of spartina grass. Behind this vegetation stand the dark outlines of hemlock, pine, and spruce trees. As you walk up the slope, moving away from the water's edge, you come across tiny clues that hint at the human inhabitants of this shifting landscape: the briefest glimpse of a towel thrown over a tree branch to dry, scented in the morning air with pine and sun, and the faint thread

of a path winding among lichen-patterned boulders. If the morning is chilly, the air carries a hint of sweet wood smoke along with the usual astringent smell of salt and seaweed.

You might come across a rustic cottage tucked into the hillside, nestled among the trees. Or perhaps you'll find a spacious abode with a soaring shed roof, wide, view-framing windows, and cedar shingles and green-painted trim that connect the house to the surrounding landscape. There could even be a rambling hundred-year-old seaside farmhouse, added on to by generations of the same family, the rhythm of the roofline undulating with gables and dormers, the first floor nearly hidden by a broad screened porch.

Regardless of the particular architectural style, a house along these turbulent shores is a bulwark against—and a refuge from—nature's might.

Well-heeled city dwellers began summering on the coast of Maine more than a century ago, traveling up from Boston, Philadelphia, and New York by train and steamer. The houses they built took inspiration from local farmhouses and fisherman's cottages clad with clapboard or shingles. Victorian architects expanded on the local vernacular, creating fanciful houses and hotels with wide shady porches, turrets and towers, fieldstone chimneys, and gable or hipped roofs.

Contemporary Maine houses often follow the shingled tradition, although with today's lofty open spaces, walls of windows, and generous decks, they are as likely to be inspired by a boat shed

OPPOSITE: *This shingle-sided Colonial home resides in Rockport, Maine, long a favorite coastal retreat. The house's architectural history is cloaked by contradictions: the roofline is half gable, half gambrel; double columns support a balcony above the front entry; an open-air patio gains shade from a view deck supported by columns with a shape most often seen on smaller, bungalow-style homes.*

BELOW: *This contemporary shingle-sided charmer borrows from past architectural traditions while incorporating the best of the new. Expansive windows, a wide, curving deck, and generous proportions meet modern needs, while softly weathered shingles and a steep-pitched roof recall earlier local residences.*

ABOVE: *Already stunning in its contemporary design, this home became even dreamier with the addition of a functioning lighthouse. The interesting columnar shape runs through the house, its glass-walled base visible below the main floor.*

RIGHT: *A barn gains new beauty and a more modern look when converted into a spacious house. Traditional materials such as cedar shingles and board-and-batten siding are juxtaposed with novel elements like soaring window columns that flank the prominent chimney and show off the strong lines of interior rafters; wide windows set into the barn's east and west walls face seaward and landward, respectively.*

or barn as by earlier residential structures. Nonetheless, the comforting touchstones of New England vernacular architecture remain. The roofs are still pitched at a dramatic angle; the central fireplaces are generously proportioned; and the cedar shingles display a silvery sheen.

Houses along the rocky shores of central California north into British Columbia often follow a more modest tradition. Recalling the isolated hunting and fishing cabins of lone explorers, the allusion here is less to history than to the wild countryside. Sitting pragmatically on pier-and-beam foundations, these houses have exterior walls sheathed in simple board-and-batten siding protected by rainproof wood stain. Above is a steep shed roof, possibly set with clear panels to take full advantage of passive solar heating. Built at the lip of the continent, these houses are imbued with a handmade aesthetic, a rugged romanticism that suits the turbulent Pacific coast.

On the islands and remote shores of the Northwest, the architecture is driven partly by the exigencies of getting materials to the site. Houses are often by necessity small, little more than artfully sculpted cubes of light and air. Flowing into one another, the living room, dining room, and kitchen comprise a single sweep of space interrupted only by a circular stairway or a simple ladder ascending to a sleeping loft. Decks, terraces, and roof decks augment the rooms, expanding living space on clear, warm days and showing off one-of-a-kind views of sky and sea.

Borrowed design traditions take root easily on these wild landscapes. European-style stone houses reminiscent of those along the coast of Brittany are particularly striking planted on a rocky shore. Golden with lichen, the thick walls echo the gray-on-gray tones of the surrounding jumble of rocks. Many of these houses are, in fact, built of stones uncovered on the property, making them appear as though they have grown naturally out of the ground. With a roof of slate or split cedar shakes, broad stone chimneys, and trim painted white or red or black, a house projects an appearance that is both bold and natural. Blocky and fortresslike, stone houses have a comforting solidity (and practical durability) in the face of the elements. At the opposite end of the architectural spectrum, Japanese designs are spare and airy, yet also blend with the natural landscape.

ON THE BLUFF

No matter how many times you walk down a familiar path, no matter how many times you crest the headlands, there's something thrilling about the sudden sight of blue water through the trees.

when it is out of sight, the sea is a powerful presence in a house balanced atop a cliff.

Cliffside houses are descendants of ancient fortresses, built for both power and safety, designed for seeing and for being seen. The basic architecture of many such houses reflects this safe-against-siege tradition. Complicated roof lines bristle with gables, cupolas, angled lookouts, cantilevered decks, and dormered windows. Opportunities abound for scoping out the view from different vantage points.

Rising out of a wooded slope, a cliffside cottage can feel like a tree house or a boat moored to the hillside with staircases and gangplanks. Picture a diminutive vacation house high above the shore, the square footprint barely ruffling the surrounding forest. Perhaps it boasts an octagonal tower room walled all around in multipaned windows—the perfect lookout spot. Cushioned built-in benches make for comfortable and space-efficient seating in the cozy room, inviting gazing, daydreaming, and private reflection. A getaway on the bluffs could also take the form of an L-shaped house overlooking a harbor; the top floor is level with the treetops, and in the crook of the layout lies a courtyard shaded with a dense mesh of living vines and paved in earthy terra-cotta tile.

When night falls, the scene morphs to include a luminous wafer of moon suspended over the dark sea. Whether you are standing at the windy zenith of gray sandstone cliffs or weathering a winter storm on a mountainous island where the relentless waves pound the rocky shores with such force that their spray rises up to a hundred feet high, you'll never feel that "edge-of-the-world" sensation more profoundly than at the top of a sea cliff.

A house perched above the surf looks both landward and seaward. It even gets two kinds of weather—hot and dry from the land, damp and cool from the sea. Days can be spent hiking as well as boating, cycling as well as swimming. The road to the house leads back through meadows and forests that have their own rhythms and delights. But even when it is out of earshot, even

BELOW: *A house with a dual nature looks to the sea on one side and to a stand of ancient evergreens on the other. The seaward side of the house is intensely vertical, with wide windows that take advantage of breathtaking* views. *The land-facing half borrows the more horizontal design of inland regions. Thoroughly contemporary in its design, the house features traditional shingles and stone, which help it blend into its wild surroundings.*

OPPOSITE, LEFT: *Striking angles and curves combine with colors that can't be ignored in an airy, private pavilion. Funky and fun, this rooftop retreat is a fine example of what an untethered imagination can create!*

OPPOSITE, RIGHT: *Every day should end this way: a relaxing lounge chair, a sip of something cold, and a lazy eye turned toward the horizon, watching the light drain away from the world.*

The best structures blend harmoniously with the sweep of ocean and the hillside topography that tumbles past them. Regardless of the styling, the architecture of these houses matches the drama of the site. Often, these homes demonstrate the severe cubism of modern design, and sport exteriors made of materials adapted from industry, such as steel and concrete. If the terrain allows, a succession of decks, joined by short flights of stairs, connects the house to the sea.

The simple, striking angles of modern architecture are especially well suited to the equally bold geometry of a sea cliff, itself an abstract collage of shapes and angles. Everything can be reduced to a few strokes: cleanly squared corners, gray concrete walls, and wide rectangular windows. Interiors are spare and restrained. Polished cement floors pigmented with color or painted in glossy deck enamel provide the little color that is needed in such a dramatic setting. Only a few large pieces of furniture are required, and a couple of oversized paintings or perhaps one or two majestically scaled pieces of primitive sculpture are the only accessories. Windows looking seaward are a shimmering curtain of glass that merges the interior and the outdoors, and are invariably left bare.

But modern architecture need not be severe—or grandiose. In the coastal Northwest, where the land falls abruptly away to the Pacific, the view is a seascape of deep coves and small islands. Fog rolls in from the ocean in huge banks, billowing over the tops of the cliffs and filling the hollows of the meadows. On bright afternoons, sunlight changes the color of the water from blue and green to incandescent gold and red. Here, the prevailing architectural philosophy is organic. Tucked into sloping hills with meadows of tall bleached grass, the houses are built of timber and stone and weathered concrete. Numerous dwellings can be cantilevered over a single wooded slope. With modern engineering and innovative designs, clusters of piers sunk into the bedrock can anchor homes to all but the most inhospitable of hillsides.

North of San Francisco in Sonoma County, a community of hillside houses called Sea Ranch sits gently in the landscape. Here, too, dwellings are planned to coincide with the natural surroundings. Design guidelines dictate everything from building materials to plumbing. The style, epitomized by the rambling, wood-sided condominiums designed in the mid-1960s by architect Charles Moore, takes its cue from the post-and-beam construction and steep shed roofs of neighboring barns. Only a few modest chimneys

Evocative of a lighthouse, this three-story tower is as much a conversation piece as it is a dwelling. Overlooking the Atlantic and set within a copse of trees, the house has been designed to accommodate both landscapes: the house's lofty third story ensures a view of the ocean without eliminating all the trees between house and shore. Unfinished tree trunks serve as posts for the porch, the cutaway third-floor balcony, and a lower-level side porch, firmly linking the structure to its forest site.

and jutting skylights interrupt the low roof lines. Roofs and walls have been allowed to weather naturally to the point that the colors blend with the nearby rocks and grassy meadows. Even the sturdy bolts and steel plates that hold the buildings together have rusted to a soft russet, and copper flashing has oxidized to a mellow green.

The homes on the coast of northern California teach architectural lessons that can be applied to any high, wild coastline. Burrowed into the slopes cascading down to the surf, these organic houses are rather like natural outcroppings. Siting is carefully planned to take advantage of special views, solar orientation, and the prevailing winds. And all this is done while disturbing as few trees as possible. Materials are chosen for their environmental responsibility: steel framing to minimize the need for lumber; treated glass to admit light while reducing heat and glare; and recycled timbers for roof beams (salvaged lumber has the added advantage of being fully seasoned and stable, as well as looking handsomely aged).

Other cliff-top dwellings are more traditional in style, and the cozy shingled cabins that hide among the trees on Maine's rocky islands and the shores of Canada's Maritime provinces are no less in tune with nature than their more modern counterparts.

Wood not only provides a natural facade that blends with the environment, but also imbues a small house with character that grows as the structures age.

SEASIDE VILLAGES

While some houses by the sea stand alone atop a windswept bluff or along a solitary stretch of beach, others gather in flocks in thriving seaside communities. Flags flutter along front porches. Pots of bright scarlet geraniums sit beside front doors. Nautical weather vanes revolve lazily in the sea breeze. A simple shopping trip down Main Street can turn into a friendly invitation to lunch on a shady porch overlooking the harbor. The village spirit is alive and well along the coast, where historic towns and a new breed of seashore development share a neighborly tradition that transcends place and time.

Coastal towns have their own special rhythm. The pace quickens at the end of May when the summer residents return. Restaurants, antiques stores, and bakeries extend their hours. Excursion boats and private yachts sit tied up at the town dock. By July, permanent residents, summer people, and day visitors happily fill the sidewalks to watch the local high school band lead a colorful parade down Main Street.

When the corn comes in, a local charitable group holds a barbecue and shrimp boil in the municipal park. On Sunday evenings, families bring lawn chairs down to the water's edge and spread out blankets to listen to a barbershop quartet singing in the Victorian bandstand. In late August dusk begins to fall earlier, and though the sun is warm, there is a new chill in the evening shadows.

Then it's Labor Day. The beaches are at capacity and the faint delicious smell of grilled hot dogs and hamburgers hangs in the air, but the following weekend the "Vacancy" signs are back up at the local bed and breakfasts. The village begins its off-season routine, turning its attention to the new school year, local elections, the business of being a town.

ABOVE: *Bungalow and shingle-style houses face the waves along the Connecticut coast. Sited close together, the homes project a sense of community as they gaze out over the quiet beachfront.*

OPPOSITE: *The quaint town of Rockport, Maine, surrounds its busy harbor . Pretty clapboard houses, shops, and churches line the streets of this traditional seaside town.*

Winter arrives, and the town celebrates the holidays with a jaunty maritime flavor: the local historical society hangs a giant wreath on the lighthouse, family Christmas trees are decorated with starfish and sand dollars. Santa Claus arrives by boat, leading a dazzlingly lit nighttime parade of fishing boats into the harbor. After Christmas, northern villages sit quiet and icebound, battened down for winter storms, as southern villages welcome a new wave of snowbirds, bringing their own lively rhythm to the streets and restaurants. Finally, spring arrives in a blaze of daffodils, and, suddenly, the yearly cycle is complete. Once again, summer has arrived.

With one foot planted on the shore and the other ankle-deep in the ocean, coastal villages share architectural styles with their inland neighbors, but transform them into an unmistakable vernacular shaped by sea, salt, and wind. By the same token, the regional architectural styles, such as the New England Cape Cod, that give seaside villages their distinctive flavor have become national styles, their elements borrowed and modernized in new construction throughout the continent.

Unlike solitary coastal homes, village houses must be good neighbors, their styles in harmony with each other, their mood in tune with the community spirit. Exterior walls, doorways, windows, fences, and gardens take on new importance on a village street. In fact, they are often dictated by community architectural guidelines. Consistency doesn't mean conformity, however. Coastal villages are

variations on a theme, charming in their range of architectural interpretations of a prevailing style, whether it is Spanish Revival, clapboard Colonial, or Caribbean tropical.

Historic Towns

America's earliest coastal town, St. Augustine, Florida, has its historic roots in Spain. Founded in 1565 by a group of Spanish explorers, it reflects the beauty of Spanish Colonial architecture, a style that has waxed and waned in popularity ever since. The architecture takes its cues not only from Spain, but from all the sunny coastlines of the Mediterranean, comfortably combining the bright colors of North Africa with the more mellow, earthy mood of

Throw a Village Banquet

Enter into the life of your town by organizing a neighborhood fete. No, you don't have to do it all yourself! Enlist your neighbors to help you throw a bash people will talk about for years to come.

▷ Be organized—to a point. Create menu guidelines but allow culinary creativity. Ask all village residents to contribute a course, be it an appetizer, entrée, or dessert. Keep track of the course contributions so you don't end up with forty-seven bundt cakes and four lobsters!

▷ A banquet is better with entertainment. Search out hidden talent among your neighbors—who knew Lois could dance the cancan; who would have guessed Neal could sing like an angel?

▷ If you decide to seat everyone at tables, don't separate the children from the adults. Keep families together, but encourage everyone to sit with folks they don't visit with often.

▷ Be flexible. Accommodate bad weather or cheerfully postpone your party until the following weekend.

▷ Invite everyone to bring their grills down to the docks. Cook up that day's catch.

▷ A stand-up banquet might be just the ticket. Let people wander from grill to grill, picking up what they like, constantly mingling.

▷ Every cook should offer copies of the recipe for whatever they're cooking.

▷ Ask everyone to pitch in a few dollars to cover expenses such as paper plates, cups, tableware. If donations are especially generous, hire an up-and-coming local magician to amaze and astound the kids and adults alike.

▷ A Fourth of July party could end in—what else—fireworks over the bay!

▷ Hold a rock-skipping contest. The best skipper could win a day of salmon fishing with a local charter service.

southern France. It is distinguished by blinding white or weathered ocher stucco walls, red clay roofs, elegant archways, shady courtyards, wrought-iron lanterns and grilles, and colorful tilework.

The style is particularly at home in the former Spanish territories of California and Florida, where oceanside towns like Santa Barbara and Palm Beach owe much of their charm to lovely Spanish-style fantasies built during the 1920s. The easy simplicity of Spanish Revival architecture and the closely related Mission style have inspired a new generation of seaside houses. The striking geometry that is the hallmark of Spanish Revival design lends itself to dramatic double-height rooms and a flowing open floor plan. The effect is enhanced by an earthy color scheme highlighted with strong sun-washed accents of cobalt blue, turquoise, apricot, sunflower yellow, and red.

The eighteenth-century coastal villages of New England gave us the famous architectural style named after Cape Cod, Massachusetts. Perhaps no single housing style is more intimately associated with coastal villages than the one-story Cape Cod, with its symmetrically placed windows and central doorway. Popular all along coastal New England, the style was well suited to the blustery winter climate, and boasted a generous chimney running up through the middle of the house. Some also featured an extension at the back; these houses are known as saltboxes because the long

sloping back roof gives them the appearance of an old-fashioned salt holder. Coastal Cape Cod houses are invariably covered in either clapboard or shingles. In frugal Yankee style, many are clad with clapboard only on the front side to reduce the need for repainting.

After the Revolutionary War, shipbuilders and wealthy merchants in towns like Wiscasset, Maine; Southport, Connecticut; and Sag Harbor, New York, commissioned new houses in the fashionable Adam or Federal style. Inspired by the designs they saw in English pattern books, American house builders constructed imposing, four-square clapboard houses with elegant front doors surrounded by pilasters, fanlights, and sidelights. Other embellishments—carved swags, garlands, urns, and medallions—echoed the natural world. These design influences continue to be embodied in new construction, updating classical idioms such as Palladian windows for today.

Perhaps the most pristine examples of historic seaport towns exist on Nantucket Island, thirty miles (48km) and a two-hour ferry ride from the Massachusetts mainland. Despite the fact that the winter population of eight thousand swells to more than forty thousand in the summer, Nantucket retains the character and architectural charm that make small coastal villages so special. Streets are still paved with cobblestones; blue hydrangeas still spill over picket fences. More than eight hundred houses built before 1850 survive, and careful

OPPOSITE: *These town houses owe their architectural inspiration to the Greek Revival, but have been elevated on stilts as a concession to the storm-ridden coast. The formal style, which embraces symmetry, is here adapted effectively for a dual-family home.*

BELOW: *Imaginative house colors, like this vibrant turquoise, are signatures of Southern beach style. Dazzling white trim and whimsical finials complete the bold look of this exquisitely symmetrical cottage.*

guidelines ensure that new construction will conform to the island's prevailing eighteenth- and nineteenth-century styles. Nantucket's lessons of scale and harmonious integration of traditional styles have influenced newer developments on both the East and West coasts.

In the 1830s, a new style emerged called Greek Revival. Essentially, this style required turning the standard New England farmhouse so that the gable end faced the street. While perfect for narrow lots found in seacoast villages, these houses needed added architectural excitement. So builders added pillared porches that imbued the houses with the look of Greek temples. The columns of a Greek Revival house reflected those found in the classical world. The simple Doric style can be recognized by its unadorned capital. The Ionic column is crowned with a capital shaped like a scroll, while the Corinthian column, the grandest of the three, is distinguished by a leafy capital. Though popular throughout the country, Greek Revival houses in seacoast towns were often sided in weathered cedar shingles instead of the conventional clapboard.

Singular Towns

At the furthest tip of Florida, where U.S. Highway 1 comes to an end, Key West has developed an architectural style all its own. Playwright Tennessee Williams once said that in Key West, "time

WAYBACK COTTAGE

OPPOSITE: *If you must take work with you, take it in style. This charming summerhouse functions as a small but breezy office, but might also be used as a reading nook or an artist's studio. Set away from the clamor of life in the main house, the space is silent and serene.*

ABOVE: *Although its total square footage is diminutive, the cottage's oversized windows, extra French doors, and vaulted ceiling help to expand the interior space.*

past remains time present." He was right. Through careful preservation efforts, the 190-block Old Town section has maintained a pre-automobile human scale, with narrow streets, narrow lots, and houses sized to match.

Like the town itself, Key West architecture—called conch style—is a blend of influences from places as diverse as New England and Cuba. A stroll through the historic district gives a nice view of shotgun houses half hidden by bougainvillea. There are Bahamian-flavored gingerbread houses with double-decker porches. And there are plain clapboard houses for homesick New Englanders, many of them designed and built by ship's carpenters drawing on their own travels for inspiration. One of Key West's most recognizable designs is the "eyebrow house," so-called because the deep, third-story front porch hangs over the second story windows. Another characteristic Key West touch: windows are often shaded with real working shutters, many hinged at the top, or jalousies— windows fitted with operable glass louvers.

Artists have always been drawn to the sea, and all over the world coastlines are dotted with modest fishing villages that have been transformed into lively colonies. Among North America's best-known examples are California's Bodega Bay and Mendocino; Cannon Beach in Oregon; Ogunquit, Maine; Provincetown, Massachusetts;

and Rockport, Texas. In these villages, the daily ritual may include an afternoon visit to the pier to watch the fishermen in their bright waterproof overalls and black boots unload the day's catch. Often, there's a path along Main Street where hardware stores and tackle shops sit side by side with brightly lit galleries and artists' supply stores. The way back home may include a side excursion along sandy streets lined with cottages whose quirky, individualistic air suits the bohemian atmosphere of the town.

A staple of these artist's colonies is the bungalow, an architectural form that originated in India as the "banggolo," an indigenous one-story dwelling. British colonials added a deep veranda to shelter the interior from the sun, and eventually adaptations of the design appeared in the seaside towns of England and North America, becoming especially popular in California. Particularly notable are the bungalows designed by architects Charles and Henry Greene, who drew inspiration from both the Arts and Crafts Movement and from the architectural styles of Japan. With its low roof line, wide eaves, clapboard or cedar shingles, and wide front porch, the friendly bungalow fits comfortably in waterfront settings—so much so, in fact, that it has been adopted by new developments such as the Third Street Cottage community, a cluster of new houses built around a village green on Washington's Whidbey Island.

The East Wharf in Madison, Connecticut, accommodates a series of boats, waiting to be put to good use. Sailing, fishing, and cruising for the sheer pleasure of being on the water are favorite activities in coastal towns, and boating themes inform everything from mailbox design to restaurant decor.

A Beach Town Renaissance

The new towns that have begun to spring up at the water's edge point the way toward redefining what it means to live in a small coastal community. The first and most influential of these new planned communities is Seaside, situated on the sugar white beaches of Florida's Gulf Coast. Mixing and matching elements of vernacular architecture from the historic coastal towns of Charleston, Savannah, and Key West, the houses of Seaside are set in a landscape of native vegetation. In keeping with a strong sense of place, special effort has been made to preserve the regional character by using indigenous plants to landscape the town.

A second generation of new communities inspired by Seaside's small-town charm (and in some cases designed by Seaside architects Andres Duany and Elizabeth Plater-Zyberk) is now establishing itself along the coast. Rosemary Beach, another community on the Florida Gulf Coast, mixes design influences of the West Indies, Charleston, and New Orleans. Windsor, near Vero Beach, Florida, has an unmistakable European flavor. Dewees Island in South Carolina is especially sensitive to the environment, limiting development to only 420 of the island's 1,206 acres (482ha).

CONQUERING THE ELEMENTS

Building with sensitivity to nature goes hand in hand with houses being able to withstand its power as much as possible. No matter what the architectural style, the house and its materials must be able to endure the relentless forces of nature.

The House's Shell

Cedar is by far the most popular coastal siding in all regions. Prized for its stability and resistant to rot and disease, it is less likely than other woods to warp or split. Milled into both clapboards and shingles, cedar is suitable for many architectural styles, from colonial to contemporary. Three varieties of cedar—western red cedar, eastern white cedar, and Alaska yellow cedar—are used for siding. All of them weather to a lovely silver gray, but of the three, western red cedar is considered the most durable and thus worth the slightly higher price. Cedar siding can be painted or stained, but purchasing clapboards and shakes that are preprimed or primed on all sides and edges before installation offers maximum protection from inclement weather.

Several manufactured materials mimic the look of traditional siding. Fiber cement, for example, can be molded to look like either shingles or clapboard. It has become popular in recent years because it won't rot or swell and, although it must be painted, it

holds paint longer than wood does. Vinyl siding is an even less expensive synthetic alternative, but because it is so susceptible to wind damage it has not been recommended for coastal locations. Recently, however, manufacturers have developed new, thicker varieties designed to lock in place that meet the exacting building codes of hurricane-prone areas, where siding must be able to withstand winds of 150 miles per hour (240kph).

Weather-Worthy Windows

Function usually takes precedence over form at the water's edge. Windows, for instance, must be able to stand up to the rigors of beach weather. In prime storm areas, windows should be reinforced with sturdy steel dividers, and large plate glass windows may be inadvisable altogether. Instead, a row of small hopper windows that tilt open to catch breezes may be a better choice. The most practical option of all is outward-opening casement windows in PVC-clad frames; the frames resist water damage and the windows, by the very nature of their construction, only grow tighter as the wind blows. Outward-swinging doors, too, are more resilient than doors that open inward.

Fortunately, traditional window styling can be combined with the latest technology. Today, it's possible to buy heat-saving,

BELOW: *In this seaward room, tall windows let in lots of sunlight and cooling breezes. Because they open outward, these windows only shut up tighter when confronted with gale-force winds off the ocean.*

RIGHT: *Multi-paned casements swing wide to welcome in a view of the Atlantic. Hardware of heavy plastic forestalls the age-old problem of corrosion, brought on by the salt air. Seashells collected from local beaches add a finishing touch to the sills.*

BELOW: *Traditional double-hung windows line the lower walls of this spacious sunroom. Note that the bottom half of each window boasts a single plate of glass for an uninterrupted view, while the upper portion features panes separated by steel muntins for extra strength. A band of eight-paned windows encircles the room at ceiling height, creating a beautiful clerestory effect and inviting the sun's rays to filter down through the trees and into the room.*

double- and even triple-glazed windows that look no different than the double-hung, true-divided windows long associated with historic architecture. A lower-cost alternative is windows that consist of large sheets of glass fitted with grilles to give them a vintage air. Snap-on grilles can be applied to both sides of the glass of a single-pane window, and can be easily removed for cleaning. On double-glazed windows, the grilles are placed between the panes of glass. Grilles are available in both plastic and wood, with the latter looking the most authentic. Regardless of the material selected it is important, for appearance's sake, that the grilles fit snugly into the inner sash frame.

Some coastal communities have exceptionally stringent building codes, designed to provide maximum protection to areas traditionally hardest hit by hurricanes. In the aftermath of Hurricane Andrew, Florida's Dade County rewrote its codes, specifying that all exterior windows and doors be protected by hurricane shutters or fitted with impact-resistant glass. Other coastal communities soon followed suit. Even if shutters and shatterproof windows are not required, it's often a good idea to look into them—when nature strikes, they can be well worth the extra cost. But just because they are functional, don't think that such shutters can't be stylish. You can select examples that have a traditional

appearance but are made of high-strength plastic or aluminum
rather than wood. Other alternatives include contemporary-style
shutters that either roll up into a roof soffit or open across a
window.

A SIMPLE PLAN

Exterior architectural style and building materials are not the only
important considerations in a beach house's design. Transitional
elements, such as doors and walkways, and a breezy interior plan
help set the tone for life at the beach.

A Welcoming Entryway

Like any home, a beach house should have an entry that signals
safe harbor to family and friends. A transition, both physical and
metaphorical, from the outside world to the inner world of the
family, the entry should welcome both residents and guests, pre-
viewing the warmth and comfort that await on the other side of
the door. A front path draws travelers forward, and may help set the
tone for the house—the path may be a formal brick or stone affair,
bordered by fountain-form sea grasses, or it may be simply a series
of log rounds or even hard-packed sand lined with an informal
edging of bleached shells.

LEFT: *A pretty painted panel, set off by a frame of stained wood, links the house solidly to its seaside site. Note the distressed appearance of the door frame; the wood may have been reclaimed from an abandoned barn, a nineteenth-century house, or even a lost ship.*

OPPOSITE: *Form still follows function, especially when it comes to entry doors that face a restless sea. Here, a pair of sturdy storm doors—outward opening and outfitted with a reinforced hook-and-eye latch—protect the more stylish inner entry doors from wild squalls. A half-round window and a book nook, above, are elegant touches.*

Sharing a House

Many families or groups of friends form "partnerships" to purchase a beach house for all to share. Make sure that these alliances go smoothly by setting some ground rules.

▷ Elect a "managing partner" annually, and let that person handle the practical details, such as keeping the books and taking care of repairs.

▷ Decide early who plans to use the house when. Keep a master schedule for the year, balancing requests from all the members.

▷ Have a "house meeting" and agree on some basic rules—the first one up makes the coffee, no wet bathing suits on the bathroom floor, everyone clears his or her own dishes, or whatever suits your gang best.

▷ Rotate chores so that necessary tasks like grocery shopping and cleanup are shared and everyone can enjoy their vacation!

▷ When the time comes to make changes in the house or in the partnership, make sure that everyone has a say.

In old-fashioned harbor towns where front yards are small and houses are spaced close together, the front door, too, is an important part of a house's personality. The step may be embedded with shells, beach stones, or colorful bits of tile and glass. The door may sport glossy paint in black, green, or red—or, if historic guidelines allow, perhaps in sunflower yellow, cobalt blue, or tangerine. On temperate summer days, the door often stands open, allowing passersby a glimpse of shadowy hall and a bright square of mirror reflecting treetops and sky.

Family-Friendly Layouts

Regardless of architectural style, beach houses face the sea. Even with the doors closed and the windows sealed tight, a house along the shore is filled with the sound of the ocean as it advances and

OPPOSITE: *Whatever the style, layout, or location of your beach house, an outdoor space is bound to be an integral part of it. This serene balcony, where simplicity and symmetry reign, serves as a sitting room in this sophisticated Mediterranean-style house. Mottled stone tiles echo the irregular patterns of the clouds, while smooth white walls mirror their color. The inviting, black iron chairs inject crisp contrast to the scene and, on a practical note, are heavy enough to stay put when the wind picks up a bit.*

BELOW: *It is generally believed that a porch should be at least eight feet (2.4m) deep in order to be comfortable for outdoor entertaining; this ample porch goes at least two feet (60cm) better. The generous expanse also provides plenty of space for daily activities. A series of wicker rockers invites lazy contemplation of the tree-lined shores.*

LEFT: *A cathedral ceiling soars above the common areas in this breezy beach cottage. Exposed support beams seem to vault into the air, providing much visual interest and a constant lesson in masterful engineering. Dining and living areas open onto one another, the conversation area defined by the placement of the sofas rather than by walls. Subtle "rooms" are also created by a change in ceiling height—the loft space, situated above the dining area, brings the ceiling there to average room height.*

LEFT: *When it's time to hide yourself away, a cozy loft is hard to beat. A comfortable chair, a good book, cheery windows—who could resist? This area is somewhat private yet remains connected to the goings on in the rooms below.*

kitchen, dining room, and living room all flow from one into another is a popular choice. Such a layout promotes togetherness, encourages lively conversation, and facilitates entertaining, all ideal in a getaway where you've come to spend time with loved ones, free of the distractions of work and the routine demands of everyday life.

Basic architectural decisions can make a house much easier to share. To keep noise under control, for instance, drywall can be hung on sound-deadening strips, and the ceiling spaces between floors insulated. In addition, the house can be zoned for different generations, with an out-of-the-way place for teenagers, preferably with TV and VCR, and other places—alcoves, nooks, and sheltered porches—for solitude. If the house is being designed with several families in mind, it may make sense to scrap the traditional master bedroom in favor of two bedrooms of equal size and with similar views.

A house where generations gather is a hard-working home. It must accommodate one couple's quiet evenings alone and a large holiday party, dressy cocktail parties as well as active children on a rainy day. Whether the style is serenely formal or carelessly casual, above all, these family homes by the sea must be tailored to the needs and wishes of the people who live there.

retreats. In the middle of the day, the rooms glow with sparkling sea light reflecting off the ceiling. Deep overhangs protect the windows, which stand open to light and air, inviting them into the house. Curtains need be no more than lightweight panels of cotton that flutter like pennants when the wind picks up as the afternoon draws to a close. Mirrors capture and reflect the shimmer of sun and water by day and the glow of candles at night. Chairs and sofas are inevitably placed in appreciation of the view.

Rambling floor plans are practical in a house created for relaxing. Interiors are laid out as uncluttered rooms that open onto each other and embrace the outdoors, making even a diminutive house feel spacious. Because beach houses tend to be favorite gathering places for friends and family, an open plan in which

CHAPTER TWO

BEACH-LOVER'S STYLE

Moods lift as soon as we cross the threshold, arms full of towels and straw hats and bags of groceries. Pieces of the outdoors start working their way inside with the first walk along the beach: a piece of driftwood, a couple of shells, a natural necklace of whelk egg cases, a dish full of pebbles, colored beach glass lined up on the window sill. These little encroaching beach things are perhaps what best define the house's decor, as the boundaries between indoors and out gracefully dissolve.

Breezy whites, ocean blues, and warm, sandy hues carried through upholstery, curtains, and paint colors also link the interior with the nearby seaside. Cushy sofas, wide windows, and easy-care floors let the house's inhabitants relax, enjoy the views, and remain unworried about household chores. Comfort and simplicity are key in a house that must be tough enough to stand up to winter storms, but welcoming to even the smallest, sandy-footed child. Whether the house is perched at the ocean's edge, riding the crest of a bluff, or hidden on the side street of an old fishing village, water is always its chief inspiration.

This sleek and sophisticated room exudes a truly genteel aura. More elegant than the typical living room by the sea, this is a space created for adults—lavish cocktail parties as well as intimate dinners take place in a world of highly polished woods, luxe fabrics, and finely wrought furniture. The sleeping couch adds a distinctly European flavor, while a long, curved wall of glass delivers panoramic views of the water.

INVITING INTERIORS

A day on and off the water often ends with relaxation indoors.
The door, propped open by day with a smooth, wave-beaten stone,
is closed against the darkness. Rain slickers and binoculars hang
from a row of hooks by the door; a bird guide rests on the table,
ready to be seized upon the glimpse of a colorful wing in the trees;
at the corners of the living room, large windows make the most of
the view; a telescope is positioned to identify passing sailboats
or the constellations twinkling in the night sky.

A beach house's interior detailing depends in part upon
where the house is located and on its particular architectural style.
In a seaside house along a wooded shoreline or atop a bluff, interior
walls may be paneled in pine, or faced with vertical beadboard or

First Impressions

Whether you have a stately Victorian hall or a modest
entryway, that first impression deserves careful thought.

▷ Change your doorbell chime to the mournful sound of
a foghorn.

▷ A boot brusher in the shape of a whale allows guests
to get rid of caked-on mud or wet sand outside before
they remove their shoes indoors.

▷ Paint the walls a warm green or terra-cotta, then
mount black-and-white photographs of the view
from your home. Adjust photograph size for the
space of the room, and strive for symmetry in
presentation.

▷ Screw mooring ties into the wall behind the door—they
make for clever coat hooks.

▷ Suspend a fishing net above the door; fill it with
glass balls, dried shells, driftwood (but don't go
overboard!).

▷ A lidded bench in the entryway can store inexpensive
slippers. Invite visitors to have a seat while they remove
their shoes, then offer them a pair of slippers for their
visit.

▷ Hang an aged, functioning barometer on the wall and
interpret it for young guests.

▷ Color schemes might echo those of the natural world
near your home. This will provide a smoother transition
from outside to inside.

▷ A small collection might find a home near the front
door. Favorite pottery pieces, for example, could reside
on shallow, densely stacked white shelves.

▷ A kid-sized lifeguard chair in the corner is sure to gener-
ate a smile and conversation.

OPPOSITE: *A wonderfully weathered front door opens to revealed a forest floor—leaves stenciled on painted wood. The random pattern of the leaves and the natural scuffing that occurs over time only enhances this floor's casual charm. Oversized shells wait in the corner to serve as door stops on breezy days.*

RIGHT: *A window seat with a decidedly nautical look provides a quiet place for reflection or needle-point. Fabrics in mixed stripes add a fresh, contemporary quality, as well as shots of color, to the wood-paneled room. Stacked trunks recall sea-going voyages, while a painting of a seaside harmonizes the whole. On the corner cabinet rests a bowl full of witches' balls—clear glass orbs filled with spidery glass webs intended to distract and trap evil spirits. These pretty amulets were particular favorites of superstitious sea captains.*

OPPOSITE: *A contemporary beach house boasts a view that has lasted for millennia. The design for the home is spare yet sophisticated, modern yet warm. Clean lines and contemporary materials—glass, metal, and smooth plasterboard—are tempered by window framing and flooring in traditional wood. The furniture likewise combines new and old: sleek shapes are executed in materials with earthy colors and textures like leather and wicker.*

BELOW: *A glossy wood floor echoes the glinting surface of the nearby sea. Wood is easy underfoot because it "gives," unlike harder surfaces like tile or stone, and has the advantage of being easily swept clean. It does have certain disadvantages, though—water can damage a polished surface and some finishes may be easily scuffed. An easy-care laminate with the look of wood may be a fine alternative for young families.*

horizontal planking. Walls and ceilings faced with wood—cedar, pine, or Douglas fir—imbue rooms with a natural warmth. When the buttery wood is left unfinished and unsealed, it ages gracefully, emitting a faint fragrance of the forest.

The choice for contemporary designs is often plasterboard painted white to establish a quiet backdrop that allows the vistas of sea, trees, and sky to take center stage. A peaked ceiling with beams painted in a slightly different hue will enliven the space, while lighting fixtures that illuminate the upper portion of the room make it seem larger than it is.

Along the sandy beaches of the mid-Atlantic, the interior walls of traditional beach houses may be whitewashed planking or conventional plaster, generally painted in pale colors that reflect the light. Bungalows on the California coast might feature Spanish-inspired stucco walls or smooth sheets of plaster.

Comfort Underfoot

The best beach house floors are those that are easiest to care for. Even indoors, wood can be painted with tough marine deck paint or bleached and left bare to age naturally. Squares of plywood or particleboard, screwed in place and finished with a high gloss, are a stylish and inexpensive alternative to conventional wood floors.

New synthetic laminate flooring, which comes in patterns that resemble wood, tile, and marble, is also practical.

Ceramic tile is another material favored for houses by the sea. A long-wearing choice for heavily trafficked areas, ceramic tile is moisture-proof and easy to clean. And though it can be chipped, tile will outlast many other materials. For beach houses, the matte or unglazed variety is best, since sandy feet can scuff and scratch glazed tile. In addition, glazed tile can be very slippery when wet.

Floors may be left bare so they are easy to sweep clean, or they might be softened with small rugs that can be carried outside and shaken when sandy footprints dry. Straw, sea grass, or sisal rugs exude a breezy informality. Sisal-look wool, however, is easier on bare feet than the real thing.

The Warmth of a Hearth

All rooms look more inviting bathed in the mingled glow of firelight and candlelight, and beach houses often feature a fireplace as a focal point. At night, the flickering light captures the gaze of family and guests, holding them in its thrall. When a crowd is gathered, the area by the hearth fills with storytelling and laughter; when just two chairs are pulled up to a welcoming fire, the talk is low and murmurous, punctuated by long, comfortable silences. With

BEACH-LOVER'S STYLE

the wind blowing through the trees and the distant surf pounding against the shore, the fireplace casts a glow that is as much emotional as it is physical, bestowing an ancient sense of peace and security. During the seasons that it is not in use, the fireplace opening can be filled with a spray of greenery, a basket of shells, or a colorful fan of coral.

Today's choices for fireplaces extend far beyond the conventional masonry examples constructed on site to include factory-built units. Less expensive prefabricated fireplaces are essentially heavily insulated boxes that can be finished with traditional brick or stone. Their limitation is that they come only in standard sizes, generally no wider than 45 inches (114cm). On the other hand, many factory-built fireplaces can be installed within inches of wooden joists. Some versions also fit into corners, while others can be placed to act as room dividers.

Typically, a fireplace mantel looks best when filled with family pictures, a jumble of shells and rocks, an old clock, a model sailboat, and any other artifacts that complement the decorative mood. If an existing mantel is less than satisfactory, it can be painted the same color as the surrounding wall to minimize its impact. Of course, a wooden mantel is usually easily replaced, so if yours is in poor shape, consider installing a new one. When it comes

to choosing a new mantel, the options are many and varied: wood, brick, native fieldstone, smooth precast concrete, and hand-carved limestone are among the favored choices.

An excellent alternative to a new mantel is a vintage one, perhaps one that has been salvaged from an old building destined for demolition. Salvaged mantels confer instant age and vintage charm, but it can sometimes be difficult to find the right fit (traditional fireplace openings are typically between 54 and 60 inches [137–152cm] high and 42 to 55 inches [107–140cm] wide). Reproduction mantels are a good alternative for historically inspired houses—manufacturers can custom size the mantel to fit, plus deliver it painted or unpainted, to be finished on site.

In lieu of the traditional hearth, many beach houses feature a wood- or pellet-burning stove. More efficient than a fireplace, a stove produces heat that is more intense and reliable. Because of this capability, a stove is a particularly wise choice if it is part of the heating plan. Americans in the nineteenth century abandoned the open hearth for the cast-iron stove, hailing it as a technological marvel. Today's wood-burning stoves are even more impressive, operating cleaner and hotter than those of just a decade ago.

Most wood stoves are made of steel or cast iron. A steel stove—generally less expensive than a cast-iron one—circulates

THE SEASIDE PALETTE

Like the changeable sea itself, beach house interiors can assume a variety of moods, and nature's inspiring palette is never far away. Or you might choose to adopt a color scheme from a faraway place that, like your own home, has an affinity for the sea.

Borrowing Nature's Hues

The colors that first come to mind for beach house decor are the serene greens and blues of ocean and sky. Picture the translucent blue-green of tumbled sea glass, the glossy emerald of an ocean wave, or the deep midnight blue of a starry summer sky. These shades are naturals for a seaside location—you might choose to carry a single color throughout the house, even if only as an accent here and there, or you might layer colors in different values of the same hue. Keep in mind one useful rule when choosing paints for beach house interiors: select a color two shades darker and two shades grayer than you think you want, because color will intensify in large doses when it is reflected from wall to wall in a sunny room. Also, note that paint will generally stand up to humidity better than wallpaper.

The neutrals of a beach on a sunny day—from the shining white of bleached shells to the earthy beige of wet sand—can also

heated air through natural convection, and is a good choice if you want to heat more than one room with it. The benefit of the cast-iron variety is that it retains heat longer, radiating warmth into the room even after the fire has burned down. A third choice, the soapstone-sided stove, retains heat even better. A variant of the freestanding stove is an insert unit, which fits snugly into an existing masonry fireplace. If you are considering this option, be aware that an old masonry chimney may need to be relined with a steel flue to handle the higher temperatures generated by inserts.

Another alternative to fireplaces and stoves that burn wood are those powered by gas. Such units come complete with decorative gas logs over and around which the firelight flickers almost as naturally as if it were consuming wood.

In a master bedroom, a British Colonial flair marks the furnishings, but the space is saved from complete formality by its airy blue and white color scheme and casual fabrics. The vaulted ceiling, painted white for extra visual height, expands the space further, while louvered doors open wide to invite in light and breezes. Confining darker colors, like the deep ocean blue of the doors, to limited spaces provides welcome accent without compromising the room's breezy quality.

work successfully, establishing a light and airy feeling, especially in a small house. Add visual interest to soothing neutrals by layering them in natural textures throughout the room, using wood, linen, cotton, and straw.

White, in particular, is a classic beach house color that never goes out of style. Plus, it has the bonus of producing all sorts of welcome optical effects. Glossy white woodwork catches the light, while rafters painted white visually raise ceiling heights. And pale floors washed with white double the amount of light reflected throughout a room. Best of all, you can employ a variety of whites in a number of different ways. In a living room, for instance, the mix might include vintage furniture washed with milk paint; plump chairs slipcovered in bright white canvas, as crisp and invigorating as a full sail; antique white ironware and enamelware; and even a bowl full of sand dollars. A mix of pieces, all in varying shades of white but with distinctly different textures and forms, will add visual interest to a bleached, clean-as-driftwood interior.

When the feeling of the interior is rustic and camplike, as in a house on a wooded shore or atop a rocky cliff, colors are likely to be dark and earthy—shades of brown, evergreen, deep red, and gold—like the natural forest surroundings. Fabrics on sofa, chairs, curtains, and accents can be informal: chintz, denim, big checks, and stripes.

The floor, comfortably scuffed, is covered—if at all—with braided rugs, threadbare Orientals, or a cheerful painted floorcloth, nothing that needs special care or even frequent vacuuming.

Old-World Colors

Of course, you might also borrow colors from other sources—the coastal regions of Greece, the Mediterranean, and North Africa have their own special shades of sea, sand, and sky. Featuring blinding whites, cobalt and marine blues, dense ochers, sunny yellows, and saturated greens, these more intense color schemes work especially well in houses with high ceilings and walls of plaster or stucco.

For old-world ambience, decorative painting techniques can be called upon to mimic the look of aged plaster. Bright yet muted, as though weathered by time, a Mediterranean palette looks stunning, particularly in combination with earthenware, ironwork, and French provincial printed fabrics.

Another inspired choice is to adopt the palette of Scandinavian houses designed to make the most of summer's brief but intense sunshine. Colors take their cues from sea and sky, and the homes are adorned with such hues as luminous yellow, buttery cream, sheer white, or seafoam green. Floorboards are bleached and walls whitewashed. Furniture is painted in shades

OPPOSITE: *Taking a cue from its Pacific Northwest setting, this house is decorated with the colors of the forest. The glow of horizontal wood paneling imbues the space with warmth, while the rug picks up the shades of evergreens and autumn leaves. The light fixture, which recalls the slag-glass and mica-shaded fixtures designed by Frank Lloyd Wright, casts a gentle radiance over the table. Shaker and Arts and Crafts designs have inspired the furnishings, which reflect an admiration for natural materials and fine craftsmanship.*

BELOW: *The somewhat industrial look of a practical desk lamp tempers the feminine flavor of this bedside tableau, even as it provides directed light for late-night reading. Simple and straightforward, the lamp highlights personal accessories, as well as a hand-woven jewelry basket that echoes the nightstand's rattan surface.*

of white, gray, and soft blue. The color scheme looks both beautiful and casually sophisticated, especially when contrasted with honey-colored pine and offset with pewter, sparkling glassware, and the natural textures of cotton and linen.

A WELL-LIGHTED PLACE

Good lighting makes all the difference in a room's ambience, and control is the key. The dining room chandelier and other hanging fixtures should be on rheostats, which allow you to alter the level of lighting easily. Reading lamps are most accommodating when outfitted with three-way bulbs, and table lamps should be positioned to banish shadows and bring seating groups together. But lamps have a lot more to offer than just the basic service of illumination. They can also be highly decorative, and are more than capable of contributing to or introducing a seaside or nautical theme. A pretty and imaginative lamp can add just the right touch of light-hearted whimsy—choose one with a funky base in the shape of a lighthouse, a ship, or even a leaping fish. Or add homespun charm to a room by filling a glass lamp base with shells you've gathered on your many walks up and down the beach. In a similar vein, you could embellish a simple lampshade with a row of tiny shells sewn around the top and bottom edges.

FRAMING THE VIEW

A beautiful view needs little assistance in the way of window treatments, and simplest is usually best. When a house sits on a shady shore or when the windows are partly hidden by porches or deep overhangs, it is all the more important to make the most of natural light with uncluttered window treatments. For the cleanest lines and best views, leave windows completely undressed. If you need privacy or to control the amount of light that enters, consider simple panels in sheer fabrics or plain cotton. Drapery tiebacks with seashell adornments help connect the indoors with the ocean

nearby. Interesting window hardware bearing a nature theme, such as cast-iron or pewter curtain-rod finials shaped like leaves, shells, or pine cones, can provide an additional link to the environment.

Sturdy shutters also help control light levels and look as good from

LEFT: *A working window masquerades as a porthole. Stained glass accented by iridescent abalone recalls the dark green depths that lie mere yards beyond the window.*

LEFT: *Like an impressionist painting, this window frames the view masterfully. The sill is just a foot (30cm) from the floor, granting a full vista. The window remains undressed, and when it is open not even muntins obstruct the view.*

ABOVE: *Gossamer swags are held in place by sea stars in a delightfully whimsical window treatment that still allows the view to shine through. Pale sea creatures painted free-hand across peach-washed walls extend the light-hearted feel.*

BELOW: *The most minimal of valances graces an impressive sweep of stepped windows lining one wall of a stairway. A garland of fresh evergreens lends a holiday air, the deep color acting as a visual anchor to the scene. Candles set into a bed of sea glass look festive enough in the daytime, but are positively breathtaking at night when lighted.*

ABOVE: *Minimal obstruction is key when framing a view. To this end, the balcony has been strung with thin steel cables rather than enclosed with traditional wooden railings. The familiar graphic shapes of Adirondack chairs punctuate the view. A clerestory lets in additional light and shows off a sunwashed upper deck.*

Movable sectional units allow this versatile sofa to be configured in any arrangement that suits the family or the occasion. Chairs flanking the towering window are ready to handle any overflow seating. Below the window stands a long hinged chest, a perfect place to stash board games, extra cotton throws, and any toys that might remain underfoot when the guests arrive.

the outside as they do from indoors. Roll-up blinds in natural reed or bamboo and basswood venetian blinds are handsome when in use and all but disappear when pulled up, especially if the window is topped with a simple swag or valance.

For houses that bask in full sun, window glass can be professionally coated with a special film to protect the interior. Consisting of a laminate of polyester and thin metal alloys, the coating deflects sunlight and the associated heat, cuts down on glare, and blocks as much as 99 percent of ultraviolet rays, which cause fabrics to fade. The best-quality films are tough and scratch resistant. Unlike earlier coatings that had a visible tint and often yellowed over time, the new ones can't be seen. Easy to maintain, treated windows can be cleaned with the same products used on ordinary window glass.

A ROOM FOR LIVING

The heart of the communal space, the living room lures adults and children alike. Facing sofas enable family members, whose on-the-go lives back in the "real world" keep them from enjoying one another's company, to get reacquainted, strengthening family ties. Comfortable armchairs provide spots to read the weekly beach-village newspaper and study nautical maps. And what better place

to curl up with a good book than a cushioned window seat with a prime view of the sea?

Beach houses are meant to be decorated free-style, so indulge yourself and fill your house with the things that feel comfortable to you. A deep sofa dressed with colorful quilts or a cozy loveseat invites people to linger. Scattered about the room, lightweight chairs—comfortably creaking wicker or airy, hoop-backed Windsors—are conveniently portable. They can be pulled up to a lively conversation circle or pushed out of the way to make space for a board game on the floor. Big pillows tempt children to lounge on the floor, and can be stacked in a corner when they aren't needed. An ottoman, roomy enough to be an extra seat or table, waits to be pulled nearer the hearth.

Slouchy, comfortable slipcovers (easy-care cotton blends or durable pure cotton work best) provide furniture with a new wardrobe, transforming formal to casual, traditional to contemporary. By visually editing a room down to a few fabrics and artful strokes of color, slipcovers help coordinate and integrate a collection of mismatched and hand-me-down furniture, usually with a relatively small investment. And they cover flaws beautifully—that purple stain from the grape juice your nephew spilled, those marks from where someone-who-shall-remain-nameless propped muddy

English country charm presides in this cozy room, with its poppy-patterned wallpaper, richly colored floral rug, and fringed, gathered draperies. Built-in bookcases lined with old favorites and cherished collectibles combine with vertically scaled windows and a multi-level ceiling to lend grandeur to the small space.

LEFT: *A collection of pillows in fabrics that share similar hues and patterns creates a comfortable spot for curling up with a book. The pillows can be rearranged for comfort, and can be added or subtracted as they wear or become victim to iced tea spills or jelly smears. The key to making a living space comfortable for a family is flexibility and the ability to cope with the accidental damage that inevitably occurs.*

BELOW: *Pieces brought down from the attic or collected from flea markets are perfectly appropriate for a beach house, where casual comfort is the chief concern. Mixing furnishings of different styles and periods creates a homey, eclectic look—here, a painted country cupboard stands easily beside a rattan armchair and a footrest draped with a plaid wool throw. A Japanese garden seat serves as an occasional table.*

feet. After a season of wet bathing suits and sandy limbs (or indeed whenever necessary), the slipcovers can be stripped off and thrown into the washing machine and dryer. For the best fit, pull them out of the dryer while they are still slightly damp and let them finish drying in place on the furniture frames.

Hand-Me-Downs and Flea Market Finds

A beach house is a perfect place for furnishings that, though old and perhaps battered, still resonate with meaning for the owners. Hand-me-downs from earlier generations can thrive in this relaxed environment. So, too, do the remnants of the older generations' childhood, including small-scale chairs and tables. Disparate

furnishings such as these that span a variety of styles can be unified with color or upholstery patterns. Old board games delight guests and make for great decorative accessories. Fabrics such as old draperies can gain a second life as place mats and napkins; vintage quilts do double duty as throws for sofas.

That round golden oak table, bought in a moment of shopping madness and stored safely out of view ever since, can find a new home as the centerpiece of the dining room. Combined with an assortment of mismatched chairs, a table such as this needs only to be refinished in a different color or painted white to assume an entirely new look. Take the same approach with an old hutch or china cabinet—you know, the one you always hated at a relatives' house and rightly feared you would inherit.

Special Treasures

A family house is often a collection of collections, filled with shared memories encapsulated in seashells, snapshots, battered oars, fishing lures, family china, and the other sentimental flotsam and jetsam accumulated over the years. Whatever they may consist of, collections please the eye, tickle the fancy, and satisfy a deep creative urge. As personal as a portrait, a collection always reveals something about the life and times of the people who gathered it,

hospitably inviting the viewer into a private world. A collection need not be grand or expensive—a basket of green and blue beach glass gathered over a lifetime of summers can mean more than a shelf full of Venetian glass selected by a designer only to round out a decorating scheme.

A collection can also be a witty comment on its collectors. Tennis rackets, golf clubs, and model sailboats speak without words about the owners' favorite pastimes. A collection brings color, pattern, and texture into an environment. Even a small grouping of objects can have impressive visual impact. In fact, less is indeed often more: a well-edited collection of a few good pieces brings more to a design scheme than an overwhelming mass of miscellaneous objects. Paintings can be propped on a mantel or sideboard, plates hung on the wall, cranberry glass or jars full of beach glass arranged on shelves in front of a window.

A proper house by the sea knows its past. In this home, a dressertop area is dedicated to local history: vintage photos of the neighboring town are thumbtacked to the wall; bottles found along the beach display native foliage.

Display Techniques

Your treasures deserve the best presentation. Try a few of these tactics.

▷ Add function to the form of your wine bottle collection. Cut off the bottoms of the bottles, then string them together with electrical cord that has bulb sockets every two feet or so (you might have to fashion this cord yourself). Add bulbs, then line your halls or private space.

▷ Create compositions of objects or artwork. Use varying heights, textures, and dimensions, and don't let the composition get cluttered. Silk flowers for dimension, baskets for texture—you get the picture!

▷ Include quirky or seemingly out-of-place elements. A bouquet of white roses with a single bright yellow rose can be lovely. An antique tabletop printing press in the family room might raise some eyebrows, but it will keep the kids entertained.

▷ A simple nail can work hard: hang a dried flower arrangement, a decorative hot pad, a needlepoint by your youngest cousin.

▷ To recall the billowing dune bracken outside, grow wheatgrass in a shallow planter. Add an occasional conch shell or bit of driftwood for visual interest.

▷ Suspend your son's model boats high over the coffee table or in front of windows (the ones without primary views).

▷ If your family size warrants, fasten old mailboxes to the wall just inside the back door, in a vertical fashion. They are a charming bit of antiquity, and make great cubbies for family members' personal effects and messages to each other.

▷ Oceanic maps can serve as intriguing inlays for glass-fronted cabinetry in the kitchen, dining room, or bathrooms.

▷ Goose and duck decoys can float along the tops of exposed beams overhead.

▷ Low-maintenance succulents are excellent showpiece plants. Grow them in rugged, cast-concrete troughs or terra-cotta pots; cluster them on a trio of reclaimed pier posts bound together with heavy sisal rope.

▷ Use a wooden cable spool as a rustic end table. Set on it an Arts and Crafts lamp, a shock of blood grass tucked into a vase, a copy of *The Old Man and the Sea*.

The Getaway Loft

The sea was made for solitude. Here's how to feather the nest where you go to be alone.

▷ Build a bench seat near a window; soften it with a custom cushion and lots of pillows with down inserts.

▷ Paint the walls, floor, and ceiling a soothing color. Or celebrate your eccentric side by painting each surface a different color!

▷ Bring in your favorite lamp for mood lighting or to help you finish off that novel.

▷ Set aside a space for pursuing your favorite hobby—be it knitting or fly-tying.

▷ If there's room, a daybed is a nice touch: there are few things more delightful than a nap in a safe haven.

▷ Cover a wall with pictures of family and friends—reminders of those who love you enough to give you some space.

▷ Display your favorite souvenirs from your travels.

▷ Install a rope ladder to lead to your interpretation of a crow's nest—safe on terra firma.

▷ Hang on the wall that quilt your grandmother made for you.

▷ Stretch out a hammock and relax.

Experimentation and an occasional change will keep a design scheme lively. (Do remember that it's best to plot out wall arrangements on paper before driving nails into the walls.) A collection is a single entity. A grouping of small photographs on the wall, for instance, is the equivalent of one large picture; a mass of candlesticks is like a single piece of sculpture.

Finishing Touches

The walls in these friendly gathering places may be covered with a collection of family photos, old maps, or watercolors of local scenes framed in museum glass. If the room is traditional in feeling, an old-fashioned curved bull's-eye mirror might hang above the mantel, reflecting the scene in one charmingly distorted view. Near a comfortable chair, a good reading lamp and a wall of books—mysteries, local guidebooks, poetry, classics, tales of the sea—are always welcome; a cupboard beneath a bookshelf or an old chest of drawers can hold stacks of jigsaw puzzles and board games.

Although entertainment in these remote houses is often spontaneous and homemade, most offer the best of both worlds by accommodating modern conveniences, too. A single, well-outfitted armoire can hold a television, a VCR, stereo components, and videotapes and CDs, all of which can be concealed behind

decorative doors when not in use. An armoire with retractable or hinged doors that fold all the way back will increase the visibility of a television screen from the sides of a room.

When it comes to providing softness underfoot, area rugs have distinct advantages over wall-to-wall carpeting. Rugs can be taken outside and shaken or beaten when you feel the need to get rid of sand or when they need a good airing after the house has been shut up. And on storm-prone coasts, they can be rolled up and put out of harm's way when floods threaten. Keep in mind that low-pile carpeting is easier to maintain than hard-to-vacuum deep pile.

RELAXED DINING

Meals at a seaside house may be taken anywhere—under the trees, out on the deck, in front of the fireplace, at the kitchen table, or bobbing across the waves in a sailboat. But often the most memorable meals are the ones shared by the whole family around a generous table. The dining room is a relaxed setting in which to savor meals and entertain company. Here the rules of etiquette, so strictly enforced at home, can be relaxed. There's no crime in placing tiny elbows on the table, whether it's a glass-topped contemporary version that enhances the airy feeling of the space or an old farm table that imparts rustic warmth.

ABOVE: *Simple and reserved, this dining area displays little superflous decoration, letting the straw-colored salt marsh take center stage. Long benches prove invaluable in seating a crowd. Don't feel the need to match every-* *thing up exactly—cheerful contrasts are part of the charm. If the mismatches are too great, you might consider unifying the pieces with a single color of paint.*

ABOVE: *Warm yellow walls, gauzy curtains, quilted seat cushions, and framed botanicals provide a fitting backdrop for this solid farm table and Shaker chairs and settee. The braided rug is soft underfoot, and can be rolled up and sent out for cleaning, an easier option for an eating area than wall-to-wall carpeting.* OPPOSITE: *A drowsy sun porch has been effectively transformed into a fresh-air dining room. Glass doors slide open to reveal wood-framed screen doors, which permit air in but keep insects out. White furniture and an array of potted and cut flowers adds to the porch-like ambience.*

In a contemporary open-plan shore house, the dining room may not be a room at all, but simply one end of a sunny multifunctional area. If there is enough space, a long farmhouse table surrounded by ladderback chairs makes a perfect setting for both family meals and rainy day projects. An extension table with many leaves is ideal for larger groups. For buffet dinners, a sideboard with storage for tableware and linens makes serving easy.

With the many comings and goings, there may be no fixed dinner hour on most days. But once or twice a week, the table is set with a colorful cloth, mismatched serving dishes, and bundles of cutlery and napkins tied with twine. The children make place cards out of smooth stones, writing the names in indelible marker. Beer and white wine chill in a galvanized tub near pitchers of iced tea and lemonade. Dessert is homemade ice cream—strawberry in

Set the Scene for a Romantic Dinner

You live on the bluff, halfway between heaven and the white surf. It's nighttime; the moon hangs in the clouds. The rest is up to you . . .

▷ Candles are a must. Try white votives in hurricane lamps, sprinkled throughout the rooms and concentrated at the dinner table.

▷ What evening would be complete without music? How about a little jazz or some soft rock? Who is your dinner guest's favorite artist? Start there.

▷ Set a pleasant table. Place a cluster of candles at the center and flank them with two small vases—each holding a single dahlia blossom.

▷ Don't be too serious! Let your playful side show through. A fun card or handwritten poem can bring a smile to your guest's face.

▷ You don't need to spend a fortune. Good wines can be had for less than $20 per bottle. Buy your vegetables and meats fresh the day of the dinner; purchase only enough for two servings.

▷ Think simple and elegant—no more than three courses. Cook the dinner yourself, staying with a recipe that you know well. This is no time for undue stress.

▷ Of course, there's nothing wrong with inviting your guest to help out by tossing the salad or serving up the blackberry cobbler.

▷ If the weather allows, serve your meal on the patio. Fresh air is a powerful aphrodisiac!

▷ A little post-dinner foot rub never hurt anyone. . . .

There's nothing like a sunset to encourage romance, and this little balcony offers an exquisite setting for a quiet dinner. It's also a lovely place to spend an hour or two in solitude.

June, peach in August—and iced watermelon. The children finish first and run out into the twilight. The grown-ups, on the other hand, sit long and comfortably in the candlelight as the dining room grows dark and the night sounds come through the door and window screens. Later in the evening, children snuggle up in soft blankets in front of the fire when it's chilly, telling ghost stories or listening to bits of family lore. On warm nights, they pitch tents under the trees, and everyone walks down to the beach to watch the light show of constellations above the ocean.

 Mismatched flatware is almost a requirement in the family house by the sea. A weekend flea market may have everything you

OPPOSITE: *Two granite-topped islands—one used as a breakfast bar and one as a work surface—dominate this sleek kitchen. Brushed steel appliances and cupboards add to the room's modern character; they also wipe clean easily, decreasing time spent on chores. On the far side of the kitchen sits a family room, the perfect spot for before- or after-dinner amusements. Through all the connected rooms glides the pervasive presence of the sea just beyond the windows.*

ABOVE: *A whimsical sense of style informs this sunlit dining area. Fifties-era beach toys and blown glass globes lend color to a table set with white stoneware. Pendant lamps sporting shades made from azure beads add dinnertime lighting when the sun has set.*

need, especially if you shop the vendors offering old silverplate forks, knives, and spoons. Many of these are sold for as little as a dollar each, with serving pieces going for slightly more.

EFFICIENT KITCHENS

The kitchen is center stage in any family house, where the day begins with the smell of morning coffee and may end with the mingled aroma of buttered corn, grilled steaks, and fresh peach cobbler. Although the kitchen is the symbolic heart of the house, in practical terms it works best if it is not actually in the middle. The more access a kitchen has to the outdoors, the easier it will be to serve the alfresco measls that are so much a part of beach living. Large windows bring seashore views to the cook and the sill provides space to display a row of shells and stones or an arrangement of feathers in a old milk bottle. Doors to the outside or to the garage make grocery hauling easier. If possible, a door that opens directly onto a deck or porch facilitates taking dishes and food outdoors and back inside.

The ideal kitchen is big enough for several cooks to work in at the same time, or if not, at least within an easy shout to the rest of the house. Two separate work zones can cut in half the time required to prepare meals and clean up afterward. A peninsula or work island supplies plenty of extra room to chop and dice, and space for a friend to pull up a stool and recap the day's activities.

An island need not be an elaborate and expensive built-in. Instead, it can be as simple as an old table with a new shelf added near the bottom or raised on casters—with brakes, of course. A central island also offers the opportunity to introduce some deco-

rative contrast: a honey-colored pine island, for instance, will warm up stark white cabinets, while a painted island can introduce a shot of color into an all-wood kitchen. The other important function served by a well-placed island is to funnel traffic and to let noncooks stay part of the action without being underfoot. To make the island function, the whole work triangle—sink-stove-refrigerator—should be on one side, with space for people on the other side so they can interact with the cook but not be in the way.

Some general measurement guidelines help avoid bumping elbows in a communal kitchen. Doorways should be at least 32 inches (81cm) wide. Work areas should have at least 48 inches (122cm) of turnaround space and, ideally, kitchens larger than 150 square feet (46m^2) should have at least 15 feet (4.6m) of wall cabinets and 16 feet (4.9m) of base cabinets. To provide plenty of workspace, the counters flanking the sink should be at least 24 inches (61cm) wide on one side and at least 18 inches (46cm) wide on the other. Somewhere in the room—on the counter or on a central island—there should be at least 3 feet (1m) of continuous counter space available for food preparation.

The Open Plan

If your house has a sunny, open configuration, the kitchen is an integral, highly visible part of the main living area. With that in mind, you'll want to make sure that its decor is in keeping with the rest of the living space.

Simple strategies can help make the kitchen visually pleasing from any vantage point. For instance, touches of color picked up from elsewhere in the house—whether they are applied in a vivid tile backsplash or echoed in a stack of bright china—can pull the different areas together.

Glass-front cabinets help maintain an airy, spacious feeling and can transform your plates and glasses into decorative objects. Because the cabinets are likely to be visible from many different parts of the house, you might opt for those with the more solid appearance of antique furniture than those with a purely utilitarian demeanor. Paint—that master of the quick change—can also be called upon to transform vintage cabinets or other kitchen furniture. A coat of paint in a color that matches or complements furniture in other living areas can instantly make your kitchen pieces part of the overall scheme .

LEFT: *This kitchen is equipped with a rear entryway located several paces away from the cooking area, an arrangement that allows room for beach toys and sports equipment just inside the door. A ladderback chair and a small desk hold stray hats, beach reading, and the like, while a wooden garden trug keeps sand buckets and shovels tidy. The kitchen's muntined glass cabinet doors echo the window and door, effectively linking the entry area and the kitchen proper.*

OPPOSITE: *A color scheme of cobalt blue and crisp white combines with charming country details in a kitchen that is as comfy as it is practical. Glass-front cabinets show off pretty glassware and collectibles, while an array of solid-front cabinets hide more utilitarian pieces. A fish-shaped hook for keys and several wooden carvings of shore birds are subtle reminders of this home's locale.*

A state-of-the-art kitchen offers all the amenities a cook could want. The oversized island houses deep double sinks that share a gooseneck faucet, and provides dining space for breakfast or a casual lunch. A commercial-style stove and stacked ovens are perfect for the serious cook, and their modern stainless-steel surface provides pleasing counterpoints to warm wood cabinetry, floors, and ceiling. Built-in spice racks stand within close reach of the cook, and an appliance garage shelters a blender, food processor, and other time-savers behind rippled glass doors.

A Place for Everything

Cabinets are one of the biggest design elements in the kitchen, and can be both beautiful and practical, bringing order to what can be a chaotic space. Faced with interesting materials, cabinets can echo the design scheme of the rest of the house—weathered barn board or pierced tin, for instance, continue a country look, while rich cherry or sleek laminate achieve a more sophisticated effect. Wood cabinets can be painted, stained, or stenciled, and old kitchen cupboards, dry sinks, armoires, and hutches can be recycled into a new kitchen scheme.

Even new cabinetry can adopt a been-there-forever look with deliberately mismatched materials and finishes. For example, one wall of cabinetry can be faced with beadboard, or a section of shelving can be finished off with crown molding.

Open or glass-fronted shelves are another popular storage option. Not only do they put pretty kitchenware on display, but they can open the space visually or provide a sense of view in a kitchen with few windows. A combination of open and closed storage works best. Necessary but less-than-beautiful dishes can go in the closed units, reserving open ones for prized possessions.

Drawers need not be conventional—a cabinet built to hold rows of pull-out baskets or colorful plastic trays provides plenty of storage. Corner storage units are a big help, especially when outfitted with lazy Susans. Roll-out shelves in lower cabinets are an easy way to hold oversized pots and serving dishes. Swing-out and pull-out shelves and racks on the back of the pantry door can triple the storage potential of a standard 36-inch (91cm)-wide closet. Even little touches can make the kitchen more fun to work in: try bright knobs and drawer pulls, perhaps with a nautical or marine motif.

Cabinets and kitchen shelving can be purchased in different sizes and configurations from home-improvement centers or may be custom made to fit your space. The latter can be a good choice for a kitchen that is small or that presents architectural challenges, because the cabinets can be designed to your exact specifications. Another option is semi-custom cabinets, which are factory made but can be ordered in a number of materials, styles, finishes, and sizes.

Practical Notes

Cooking in a kitchen by the sea usually involves feeding a crowd, and, more often than not, menus feature lobsters, crabs, corn on the cob, and other delicacies requiring unwieldy pots. A stove big enough to handle giant pots and skillets makes cooking and cleanup easier.

OPPOSITE: *A kitchen by the sea can be the perfect repository for all those pieces that don't match the good dishes or aren't quite up to use in a more formal setting. Stick to a color theme—here the ever-popular blue and white—and the pieces will look charmingly mismatched rather than simply jumbled.*

RIGHT: *Seashells make clever and decorative tablecloth weights. Gather the shells from the beach, soak them in water with a few drops of bleach added, and glue them to ribbons or raffia. Drop lead fishing weights into chambered shells for extra heft.*

If your house typically hosts large gatherings, you might consider installing two dishwashers and two refrigerators. A side-by-side refrigerator is the easiest type for children to open and close, allowing a thankful measure of independence; ice and water dispensers incorporated into the refrigerator door are a convenience for everyone. A second refrigerator or freezer need not be housed in the kitchen itself—it may be possible to borrow space from an adjacent pantry or a nearby utility room.

Time-saving appliances installed using space-saving strategies are part of a well-designed kitchen. A microwave oven can fit above the range, for instance, to save cabinet and counter space, while a water filtration system added beneath the sink eliminates the need to store bulky bottled water. Super-sized fixtures such as a generous sink with a gooseneck faucet allows cooks to fill those big lobster pots with ease.

Good lighting, too, is an essential part of a functional kitchen, but take care that it isn't too harsh. Even the most beautiful of kitchen designs falls apart under the glare of a powerful fluorescent fixture. Ambient lighting is important, especially if it is supplemented with well-placed task lighting that adds personality as well as illumination. Instead of selecting a conventional under-cabinet fixture, further the seaside theme by choosing a small shell-encrusted lamp for the counter. Or shop for a chandelier in a nautical theme—one with bobbing paper sailboats, for example, that you can hang above the breakfast table. A ship's lantern above the sink brightens a kitchen, whether the lamp is on or off.

Hardworking kitchen floors needn't to be purely utilitarian; modern finishes are tough and easy to maintain, and virtually any material from wood to concrete makes sense in a kitchen by the sea. The floor can convey the decorative mood—concrete, brick, or terra-cotta, for instance, has an earthy look, while plank floorboards or checkerboard tiles suggest a vintage country style (placed on the diagonal, a traditional checkerboard pattern is particularly striking). Wooden floors can be painted or stained with a pattern; tile and vinyl ones can be inset with a rectangle of patterned tiles to create a "rug" that never needs straightening.

One final practical concern is safety, especially important in a family kitchen. Utensils and supplies that children use often should be kept in an easy-to-reach spot. Heavy items are best stored

*Be creative when designing center-
pieces for your table. This display
features an array of seaside treasures—
conches, scallops, sea urchins, and
even a sea horse—on a serving tray.
Wayside flowers complement the
ocean's offering.*

in low cabinets or in ones so high that they are out of children's reach. Children especially enjoy having a pull-out work counter at their own height; as an alternative, fit a plastic tray snugly in an open drawer. Nonskid floors are safest for everyone in the family, but especially for the youngest and oldest members. Touch-latch doors are easiest for children to open, and are less likely to catch little fingers. Equipping one cabinet with a lock keeps toxic cleaning supplies and other dangerous kitchen items out of children's hands.

Don't Forget the Details

Decorative details are as striking in a kitchen as in other areas of the house, but are sometimes neglected in this most utilitarian room. Decoration can be simple and comfortable, making good use of items accumulated over many summers and by different generations. Navigational maps and posters of local birds or game fish are easily thumb-tacked to the wall. An old school blackboard and a teacup full of chalk sits by the kitchen door, awaiting family members who want to leave messages.

Turned on its side, a vintage wooden soda-bottle carton becomes a handy storage unit, while open shelves of reclaimed boards, washed with a thin glaze of color or left natural, hold colorful china and glassware. Blue-and-white enameled camping cups are vases waiting to be filled with bunches of the season's fresh herbs. So, too, is a battered coffee pot, brimming with an impromptu bouquet of wildflowers.

The backsplash between the counter top and the upper cabinets is a particularly opportune place to create design impact without breaking the budget. The wall can be painted to contrast with the rest of the room or may be embellished with decorative painting. Dressing this space up with hand-painted ceramic tiles— even a few scattered among less expensive solid-color ones—creates a striking accent.

Many kitchens have a soffit between the cabinets and the ceiling that can be a great showcase for art works, porcelain plates, or other decorative accents. By adding a stenciled design or favorite motto or literary phrase, the soffit becomes a work of art itself.

PRIVATE RETREATS

There is a special tranquillity found in a bedroom near the shore. At night, lying in bed, you hear such sounds as a distant foghorn rolling across the water and bell buoys clanging gently in the incoming tide.

Furniture is spare and breezy, as compact as a ship's cabin, with built-in cupboards, leggy little nightstands, and perhaps a rocking chair and a trunk. Take the same relaxed approach in

The graphic silhouette of a butterfly chair graces a serene bedroom balcony. A fine mesh screen prevents insects from entering, but lets the salt air permeate the room. Colors are neutral or muted to enhance the feelings of peace inspired by the fine view.

BELOW: *Strong geometry and natural materials are predominant themes in this restful bedroom. A small fireplace, light-filled window seat, comfy bed, and private entrance make this room a haven even when the house is full.*

OPPOSITE: *A white-on-white scheme is broken only by sandy neutrals for a supremely soothing effect. High wainscoting draws the eye toward tall windows that open from the bottom,* *allowing great cross-ventilation. Roman shades screen the sun and provide privacy when necessary. The ultimate indulgence is a light snack enjoyed in bed.*

decorating the more private areas of a beach house that you've adopted for the gathering places.

Bedrooms make excellent sanctuaries for the treasures of childhood, and some furniture can be successfully recycled, eliminating the need to purchase a whole new set. Consider installing in a guest room or child's bedroom the bed you owned growing up, its headboard scuffed from childhood rowdiness and sleepovers with best friends. Your old red wagon is now a great storage space

for stacks of books. Even old high school yearbooks can imbue a room with added character and a sense of personal history.

The Master Bedroom

The view from the bedroom windows—a grand vista of the ocean-side—is the first you see in the morning and the last you see at night. The surroundings are worth contemplating, so treat windows with care. In the bedroom of a traditional shingled house, a pair

BELOW: *The sinuous lines of a sleigh bed and a curving night table complement the bolder, heavier shapes of the Arts and Crafts desk, chair, and bureau, lending an airier feel to a room that might seem ponderous if filled exclusively with weighty Mission pieces. A clerestory and plentiful lower windows are essential to brighten the dark wood paneling and furnishings.*

OPPOSITE: *While the centerpiece of this room is also a sleigh bed, the space achieves a completely different look thanks to cathedral ceilings, silk-draped French doors, pristine white walls, and mounds of snowy white, eyelet-edged bed linens. A framed mirror with an elegant beveled edge doubles the view and adds visual depth to the room; painted hatboxes, framed photographs, and perfume bottles are pretty personal touches.*

of chintz-covered chairs might sit conversationally in a windowed corner, the view framed by long, white cotton curtains pulled back to reveal treetops or ocean. Matchstick and narrow-slatted wooden blinds are also attractive, and offer excellent sun control. In a tropical climate, where the morning light filters indoors through the luminous giant leaves of a banana tree, tall shutters that fold back are simple and practical. For some fortunate homeowners, French doors lead from the bedroom to a balcony furnished with café chairs and a table just big enough for morning coffee.

Handsome window dressings don't have to be expensive or elaborate. Curtains fashioned from inexpensive muslin or even from dainty flea market linens can be more welcoming than brocade in a casual summer bedroom. Narrow windows can be made to seem larger by extending curtains beyond either side of the frame. Where privacy is not a concern, curtains need not close, creating an opportunity to indulge in more expensive fabrics for the narrow panels.

The bed itself is worth a splurge. In a white clapboard house overlooking a cove where sailboats bob in the tide, a master bedroom might be appropriately furnished with a traditional eighteenth-century four-poster dressed in monogrammed linens. In a grander home, a mahogany sleigh bed outfitted with a crisp white bedspread might be just the right focal point. An iron four-poster hung

Making the Most of Your Space

If your seaside getaway is fighting the battle of the bulging closets, read on. You might be surprised to discover where storage opportunities lie.

▷ **Consolidate.** If your seaside home is a vacation retreat, examine your wardrobe there. Do you really need two jackets, three hats, four pairs of shoes?

▷ **Throw away or sell any item you haven't used in the past two years.** Chances are, you never will.

▷ **Know your home's "voids."** That dead space under the stairs could be fashioned into a miniature closet with a small door and a driftwood pull.

▷ **Window seats** are a prime spot for installing shallow drawers or cupboards.

▷ **Examine your wall space** for empty real estate on which to hang shelves.

▷ **Make your room decorations do double duty as storage:** a coffee table with drawers, a miniature boat upended and filled with shelves—you get the idea.

▷ **Invest in a closet management system** to take advantage of every last square inch of available space.

▷ **In its corners,** virtually every room offers four opportunities for storage. Corner shelving is available; corner display cabinets are another option.

▷ **If you haven't built your seaside getaway yet,** be sure your plan incorporates plenty of storage space.

▷ **You can always fall back on under-the-bed storage boxes!**

with light muslin draperies—reminiscent of mosquito netting—is cool and inviting in a modern house inspired by the classic simplicity of a Caribbean home. An old iron bedstead, snared at a flea market and spray-painted white, makes a simple and charming addition to more modest bedrooms. When storage is tight, a space-efficient option is a contemporary platform bed that includes under-the-bed drawers. Also, many housewares stores sell boxes that roll beneath the bed for keeping various accoutrements out of the way.

Amenities are delightfully utilitarian: a wicker laundry basket to hold fresh towels, a mirror leaning at a slight angle to catch a piece of window and sky, a shelf for summer reading. Clothing needs are minimal, so a small closet or even just a row of hooks will often do. Striped wool blankets or a goosedown comforter for chilly nights can simply lie folded at the foot of the bed.

Guest Rooms

Family houses are designed for comings and goings. Over the generations a single house may multiply into a compound, a tiny village of several cottages, or a main house with guest cabins scattered nearby. The indoor-outdoor nature of seaside life means that guest rooms and guest cabins can be small and simple, but they need not be austere. Small bedrooms are perfect for

experimenting with color. They can be painted in vibrant colors—rose-petal pink, leaf green, French blue, deep golden yellow—that might be too intense in larger doses. A good bedside light, a comfortable chair, a dresser, a place to put away suitcases, and a couple of books—paperbacks, so that guests can take them if they haven't finished with them by the end of the visit—go a long way toward making a guest room comfortable.

ABOVE: *A waterfront home can be a sentimental vault. This guest room is furnished with hand-me-downs from family members—including the iron bed and bedclothes and the oak dresser and mirror. The water pitcher and bowl on the dresser add to the vintage spirit of the room.*

OPPOSITE: *The ambience of a cabin fills this beachfront bedroom, where a checkered quilt and checked and striped pillows add a touch of nostalgia. Vintage quilts and linens fill a reclaimed kitchen cupboard, an unusual but pretty and effective way to store textiles. Exposed rafters, wood walls and floors, and simple frame windows complement the rustic atmosphere.*

Guest quarters can be supplemented with sleep sofas, which have improved dramatically in the last few years with the advent of specially designed innerspring mattresses and more convenient operating mechanisms. The options have multiplied as well. If there is not space for a conventional sleep sofa, it may still be possible to accommodate an extra guest or two with a sleeper built into a loveseat or a roomy chair-and-a-half. It's worth paying extra for quality: construction should include a crossbar—recessed at least 2 inches (5cm)—to give the mattress support across the middle; mechanisms that are stepped back from the side of the mattress when the bed is open to avoid snags; and an innerspring mattress that is at least 5 inches (12cm) deep.

Activities with the Kids

Children love to explore and create. Get their eager minds buzzing with these fun activities.

▷ Sleep with the dunes. Bring a tent or pitch a lean-to against a mound of driftwood.

▷ Go "saling"—garage saling, that is. Pick up old vases for a song, grab the glue gun, and decorate them with seashells and translucent rocks. Soak the sea's treasures in a weak bleach solution to remove unwanted odors and clean off any residue that would prevent the glue from adhering well.

▷ Take a hike, with the young ones as guides. Let them make the rules; let them decide where to go. Change their course only if they choose an unsafe path.

▷ Sand castles, of course. But don't forget sand *monsters*— grainy creations fettered only by the kids' imaginations!

▷ Sneak out at midnight and bury a plastic food-storage container full of loose change, then dream up a list of clues to lead your young treasure-hunters to the bounty.

▷ Discover the natural world. Go for a walk and try to find as many unusual plants, animals, and rocks as possible. Spend an afternoon identifying them in field guides.

▷ Include the kids in light maintenance tasks. Children can be incredibly conscientious, so put paintbrushes in their hands and have them take care of the window trim.

▷ Get them wet. Give them snorkeling gear and release your young Cousteaus to the ocean (with adult supervision, of course).

▷ A scavenger hunt never fails. Mix the easier finds (scallop shell, bull kelp) with more challenging objects, such as a whole sand dollar or human-shaped chunk of driftwood.

▷ Fashion driftwood pieces into wind chimes—it won't matter if they don't ring

An interesting mix of tradition and innovation prevails in this quaint bathroom. Wainscoting is an old-style touch, as is the picture rail, which provides a clever spot for small toiletries and display items. The stainless steel sink and sculptural water pipes verge on the avant-garde, while a wire mesh basket learns a new trick when tacked to the wall and used as a towel holder.

Children's Rooms

Children love the sleepover adventure of bunking together in a vacation house. Bunk beds and trundle beds expand the sleeping options without taking up precious floor space. A sleeping bag or two stored in the closet creates space for even more overnight guests.

A child's room is a good place for a little whimsy—floors and walls stenciled with sailboats or cockleshells or bits of seagoing poetry. Elements of several store-bought stencils can easily be combined to make a fresh new design, or a totally new design can be created using clear acetate sheets and a craft knife. Amateur artists who are not comfortable drawing freehand can find a picture they like and enlarge it or reduce it on a copy machine before transferring it to the stencil. Or children can decorate their own walls. Paint one section with blackboard paint and provide a plastic sand bucket filled with many different colored chalks.

Baskets or bright plastic tubs help make toy cleanup easy; in addition, children will appreciate having their own storage place, even if it is no more than a wire basket or a small trunk. A row of hooks along one wall for clothes will help keep the bedroom neat without the fuss of a closet. A folding screen provides privacy, if wanted, and helps hide clutter. If covered with fabric, a folding screen can double as a bulletin board for pinning up postcards and holiday artwork.

BATHS

Beach house bathrooms run the gamut from tiny, functional spaces to elegant, spalike retreats. Often a luxurious master bath is supplemented by a more modest bathroom for guests or kids and a powder room or two, depending on the size of the house and the usual number of occupants.

The master bathroom might serve as an elaborate spa, complete with soaking tub, a Jacuzzi, or even a sauna. A heater installed in the ceiling is also much-appreciated in those chilly after-shower moments. Wide counters of smooth, cool marble or homey tile inset with double sinks are a welcome indulgence, as are full-length mirrors. If space allows, include an armchair for extra comfort and an occasional table to hold bath salts and good tub reading.

The most beautiful of master baths are positioned to take advantage of sea views, conjuring the image of bathing in the

Decorative Tips for the Bath

Master bath, everyone's bath—any type of bath deserves a unique look.

▷ Go "marine": fasten genuine portholes to the walls, set into tongue-and-groove beadboard from floor to ceiling.

▷ Place wicker bowls of seashell-shaped soaps in a random pattern throughout the bath.

▷ Create a glass-bottom-boat illusion with trompe l'oeil paintings of dolphins, crabs, fish, and other sea creatures on a deep blue floor. Cover the paintings with several coats of polyurethane for a three-dimensional feel. Set a dried starfish in a corner to startle inquisitive fingers!

▷ Install a whirlpool bath in a bay window with a view of the sea, and enjoy frothy waves on a small scale.

▷ A lobster box can hold towels and robes; crab traps can corral your toiletries and soaps.

▷ If there's room, a comfortable chair is nice: your sweetheart can chat with you while you take your Saturday night bath.

▷ Line the tub with plants. Be sure to include ferns and flowering bulbs such as bold tulips and paperwhite narcissi.

▷ Storage choices can be eclectic yet pragmatic: an armoire, a bookcase, even a baker's rack will serve.

▷ Lay down a thick area rug bursting with hues that complement your color scheme and laced with maritime patterns to evoke the sea.

▷ A jade chess set looks good next to the tub and just might come in handy if anyone cares to join you for a soak and a game.

▷ Your faucet handles can be miniature replicas of mighty ships' wheels. Sprinkle tiny collected shells along the back side of the tub's edge.

▷ Colorful ship flags make a eye-catching upper border for the shower curtain.

A pyramidal alcove houses a roomy whirlpool tub in a space perfectly suited for long, luxurious soaks. Generous windows on two sides offer wide views of the sea. At night, numerous skylights invite stargazing.

ABOVE: *Mosaic tile depicting a sailfish and its shadow enlivens the shower and tub in this playful bathroom. A glass block window admits plenty of light to wake up recalcitrant risers. In the corner, exotic blooms look eerily like deep sea sponges.*

OPPOSITE: *Marble tiles and countertops and a lavatory of bleached wood confer a feeling of opulence to this lavish master bath. A deep spa tub is tucked into a wall of glass—only a thin pane separates the bather from the white sand and rolling blue sea.*

ABOVE RIGHT: *A wood-framed window opens wide so the bather can enjoy an unobstructed view of the beach. Chrome handles set into the side provide solid grips for getting in and out, an important consideration when the front tub ledge is this wide.*

roiling waves. Some such spaces may even open onto the outdoors, providing an incomparable feeling of air and light.

Other bathrooms in the house may be less opulent but should be no less comfortable. Provide guests with plenty of fluffy towels and a basket of toiletries, such as shampoo, fragrant shower gel, and moisturizer, especially important after a day in the sun and saltwater.

Control bathroom clutter with small accessories like colorful cups for toothbrushes and rows of decorative hooks to keep wet towels and clothing off the floor. It is much easier to keep track of linens if the towels and washcloths are color coded by room. Cleaning can be streamlined even further by putting towel bars or portable towel racks in children's bedrooms and making them responsible for their own bath linens.

CHAPTER THREE

THE PLEASURES OF SEASIDE LIVING

The beach is a busy neighborhood.

Shore birds nest in the grass of the dunes, and colonies of barnacles cling to the wet pilings of docks and piers. Tidal pools teem with sea stars, horseshoe crabs, and other ocean denizens. In the damp darkness beneath the sand, clams go about their quiet business.

Wake early and walk down to the water's edge to appreciate the morning activity, or sit on the deck with a cup of fresh coffee and watch the clouds lighten from deep purple to pink to yellow to white. Sunny afternoons are for lazing on the sand with a novel or swimming in the brisk, salty sea. Even blustery weather has its pleasures: the sharp wind that sweeps the beach after a northeastern storm whips the gray water into spumy waves, bringing treasures forth from the deep.

In addition to these quiet pleasures, there are more boisterous affairs to enjoy. Everyone anticipates the annual events: the Fourth of July picnic, blueberry picking, and the community oyster roast down on the beach. And, lest anyone forget, there are clambakes to look forward to as well as the family's traditional Labor Day boiled lobster dinner, the official end of the season.

A comfy hammock in sunny Provençal colors is perfectly positioned to take advantage of ocean breezes. The rattan occasional table holds within arm's reach the accoutrements of a lazy afternoon—sunglasses, a good book, a light snack.

A Picnic on the Beach

A weekend lunch is better with the surf as your symphony. Grab the basket and go.

▷ Let's face it: you will have to deal with wind. If you bring a blanket, pin down the corners with driftwood or rocks.

▷ A traditional reed picnic basket may be pleasing to the eye, but it will let sand blow in. Instead, carry your goodies in a canvas bag.

▷ A parasol is a must—look for one with a high SPF (sun protection factor) rating. Stake it deeply and let it shield you from the sun and wind.

▷ A transistor radio might be nice to have along, but for background music, it's hard to beat the rolling waves.

▷ Find an abandoned rowboat (preferably wood) and set up your meal in it.

▷ The meal setting may be practical, but it can still be elegant. Tuck your tableware into organza sleeves. Colorful acrylic plates and cups resist breaking. Add a tuberose posy for a whimsical centerpiece.

▷ Let's eat! Cold cuts sandwiched between sourdough rolls, fresh fruit, your favorite pasta salad (toss in some crab meat for added zest), a mixed-greens salad for color and great taste, turnovers for dessert.

▷ A fruity wine, such as a Johannesburg Riesling, will suit your light lunch perfectly.

▷ If local regulations allow, light a driftwood fire and simmer a pot of seafood stew or mussel soup.

▷ The perfect ending to a perfect outing: read a little Pat Conroy to your lunch partner—perhaps something from *The Prince of Tides*?

This brick patio, just a short walk from the water's edge, functions as a fresh-air breakfast room. An early-morning swim or walk along the beach invariably ends with bagels and a fruit salad served in cheery bowls. Cushioned wicker chairs cradle diners comfortably, while a glass top on the table alleviates the need for a tablecloth, which can be problematic on windy days.

Life at the beach is mostly about life out-of-doors, and thanks to our outdoor rooms—our porches and decks, as well as our seaside gardens—we can participate in this life most fully.

THE GRACIOUS PORCH

A porch allows you to bask in the splendor of the natural setting, while retaining all the conveniences of home. Whether open-air or screened, it extends the functional space of your home, serving as an outdoor living area.

The simple but strong architectural bones of this screened porch are its chief ornament. White-painted rafters expose cedar shingles from the underside, while columns, supplemented by square beams, serve as supports. Amply cushioned rockers and one small table are all that are needed to make this porch an ideal place to view daily sea-changes.

OPPOSITE: *This lanai, with its low, squared-off walls, incorporates boxy teak furniture that blends seamlessly with the lines of the space. Upholstery and pillows in a rich cocoa color continue the earthy theme set by terra-cotta-colored walls and beige stone flooring.*

RIGHT: *The geometries of the lanai have also been applied to the garden and adjacent terraces. Grass grows low between prominent, square-cut flagstones. Massive raised planting beds echo the angular terra-cotta walls of the lanai and frame the path to a patio and more garden treasures in the distance.*

When it comes to decorating the porch, the surrounding scenery is the best ornament there is. A breathtaking backdrop might be enhanced with hanging baskets of cascading blooms or perhaps some galvanized steel buckets filled with wildflowers or creamy hydrangeas. Such natural adornments will serve as links between the porch and the landscape beyond.

Wide overhangs—traditional features found in such regions as New England and the Deep South—keep porches dry enough for children to play outdoors even when it's raining. Water drips from the eaves as the rain beats a steady rhythm on the roof overhead. At other times, overhangs shield windows from direct sun and help keep rooms cool during the heat of the day. If one side of the porch is too sunny in the morning or afternoon, shades can be called into action. These come in all sorts of forms, from wide matchstick blinds that can be lowered and raised at will to simple white cotton curtains that can be tied back with a heavy cord when not needed. Besides regulating the amount of light that enters the porch, these practical touches help create a sense of privacy.

A large wraparound or L-shaped porch provides the opportunity to divide the space into separate "rooms." One wing might function as a living room, while the other serves as a dining room. Or one side might be furnished as a gathering area for entertaining friends and family, while the balance of the space is reserved for a private sitting area. Generously proportioned chairs and sofas are easily arranged to create a destination for a sociable group looking for a place to retreat and relax. At the far end of the porch, a pair of high-back cushioned chairs or a rocking settee could delineate a corner conversation area just for two.

When the stickiness of a still and humid day descends, a ceiling fan on the porch is sure to be appreciated. And for nostalgic appeal as well as comfort, fill a wicker basket with vintage hand-held fans and place it close to the sitting area. Tradition calls for a porch ceiling painted sky blue or green—a legacy of the days when those shades were treated with arsenic to repel insects.

BEACH HOUSE DECKS

A modern house is more likely to have a deck than a porch, but it may be completely open and unsheltered, partly roofed, or protected by a pergola. A beach house deck—whether a

straightforward rectangular design of treated timbers or a high-style assemblage of nautical curves and angles—is more than a place to enjoy an evening drink or an afternoon sunbath. Well planned, it can beautifully extend and enhance the proportions of the exterior. Plus, it effectively increases living space.

Some clever architects set the deck off to one side of the house instead of affixing it to the front, where it might interfere with the view from the inside. If a deck does run across the beach side, the traditional wooden railing can be replaced with one in a less obtrusive material, such as stainless steel. Decks close to the ground can often be protected with nothing more than a wrap-around bench.

For safety's sake, deck railings should be 42 inches (107cm) high. Some municipalities have tightened their restrictions further, requiring that the gap between vertical or horizontal rails be no more than four inches (10cm). To minimize the visual intrusion of so many rails, architects increasingly specify strong thin railings of wrought iron, steel pipe, aluminum, or even stainless steel cable. Panels of tempered glass are an alternative, though the salt spray and sea air can cause them to cloud up eventually. Rope or fabric netting are generally not considered appropriate because they can rot and give way under pressure.

No railing is required when a deck sits just a step off the ground. Tangles of wild roses and convovulus planted around the deck will lap at its edges, and pots of rosemary and basil can grow in a protected corner beside the door. An awning or overhang above the deck is a good idea, for it will provide cooling shade that makes relaxing outdoors comfortable, even in the heat of midday. Retractable canvas awnings can offer shelter during the hottest part of the afternoon and be folded closed when the sun is sinking in the sky. Such protective devices come in all sorts of colors and patterns—you might opt for a solid blue that echoes the sea or for cheerful stripes that recall the festive look of a beach resort.

At night a deck can be brightened by tin lanterns, old-fashioned trainmen's lamps, or, on a still evening, a row of tealights cupped in mussel shells. The lemony scent of citronella candles defines summer. Bring citronella votives out onto the deck, or plant a handful of citronella tapers in a bucket of sand. The wonderful thing about soft candlelight is that it won't blind you to the view. You'll still be able to enjoy the wide band of wet sand shining in the afterglow of sunset, the braided channels left by the retreating tide, the shallow pools ruffled by the evening breeze, and the willets and sanderlings running along the water's edge. In the distance, perhaps you'll spot a single fisherman enjoying the meditative

Glowing aquamarine in the sunset, this pool presents a tempting alternative to a salt-water swim. Wide decking, ample seating, and a view to cherish make this an ideal spot for a party. The comfy lounges and armchairs feature cushions covered in the latest easy-care, drip-dry fabrics.

rhythm of surf fishing, casting and reeling, casting and reeling as the evening shadows lengthen.

FURNISHING THE OUT-OF-DOORS

At the shore, outdoor furniture is more than an afterthought, it's a vital piece of the home's outfittings—after all, you've come to the beach to spend time outside. Plus, porches and decks are often highly visible from the beach, and you'll want to make yours a pleasing part of the view.

Classic Beach Furniture

Seating possibilities run the gamut from wicker chairs to rockers to enticing chaise longues. Picture a group of rocking chairs lined up in a row to give their occupants a fabulous view of the sea. These chairs might all be of the same style but painted in different hues to create a colorful display. On a small porch or deck, where space is tight, built-in benches can provide streamlined seating. Cushioned for comfort, the seats of these benches are often hinged, opening up to hidden storage space.

A daybed draped with quilts and a cover of crisp striped ticking is another beautiful option for a porch or a deck with protection from the elements. And of course, what could be more alluring

THE PLEASURES OF SEASIDE LIVING

than a painted porch swing—the perfect spot in which to linger during the early morning or the long blue hours of twilight. For extra seating when friends drop by, you might keep a couple of old wooden chairs, light enough to carry out to the porch, in the kitchen.

Chairs should be arranged around a coffee table or placed beside occasional tables so that friends and family have a place to set their drinks, snacks, books, and crossword puzzles. A group of chairs set around a table also provides the opportunity to play board games and cards out on the porch or deck. If space permits, there might even be a dining table on the porch as well.

No matter what the style of a beach house, classic outdoor furniture is never out of place. And what could be more classic than a row of Adirondack chairs, situated to take in the view? Keep in mind that those with back wheels and hand grips are easiest to move indoors for the winter.

Wicker is another great choice for the shore. Just make sure that you choose the "all-weather" variety, which is finished with a durable protective coating that will, for the most part, stand up to the elements. Wicker pieces are easy to clean, but may require touch-ups and periodic refreshing with a new protective coat if kept in a fully exposed location. Black is an unusual selection that harks back to the Victorian Age. It's also an eye-catching

alternative to the more traditional white or clear-finished wicker, and is especially appealing on porches that are highly visible from the indoors. Forest green is another pleasing option and, like black, doesn't show dirt as easily as white.

Cast- or wrought-iron outdoor furniture is a nostalgic choice that looks particularly lovely on an old-fashioned porch. A distinct advantage to these heavy metal pieces is that their weight will keep them securely in place when the wind picks up. Iron can leave rusty footprints on stone or concrete surfaces, but it is easy to protect a deck by putting small plastic devices—available at hardware stores and home centers—under metal furniture legs. Any furniture selected for a beach deck should have style and durability, yet should also be devoid of metal details and fasteners such as bolts that might rust and leave streaks.

Teak, the same wood favored for sailing ships, has come back into favor in recent years. A dense tropical hardwood rich with natural oils that protect it from decay, teak weathers over time to a soft gray. On shipboard, teak is varnished and polished, but furniture makers recommend no more than the lightest maintenance. Spraying teak pieces every week or so with a high-pressure garden hose washes away pollution without loosening the joints.

Fabrics for All Weathers

With the recent innovations in outdoor fabric construction, it is easy to dress deck furniture in style. Many outdoor furniture sets come with cushions and umbrellas covered in acrylic, a synthetic fabric that is available in all sorts of hues and patterns. Prints are dyed with special pigments, similar to those found in house and car paint, that are UV-resistant and rated to last five times longer than conventional dyes. You can expect even longer service out of acrylics that boast solids, stripes, and jacquards, because these fabrics are "solution dyed," which means that the pigment is added while the acrylic is still in liquid form. Thus, each fiber is colored all the way through.

Inherently sturdy, stain resistant, and mildew resistant, acrylic fabric requires little care. Printed acrylic can be cleaned with a solution of one cup (250ml) of mild detergent to three gallons (12l) of water, while solution-dyed acrylic requires one cup (250ml)

OPPOSITE: *A glass-topped dining table with a metal frame echoes the glassy surface of the water beyond. Set with shell-shaped dishes and simple glass-ware, this table is ready for a festive summer repast. Folding garden chairs and the butterfly chairs beyond can both be moved indoors easily when a storm blows in. The table, too, would need to be protected in a heavy storm, as its glass top is vulnerable to flying debris.*

BELOW: *This outdoor shower, with both a door and a shower curtain for privacy, allows guests to rinse off sand and salt before entering the house. The area also provides space to stash sports equipment, towels, and wet swim suits.*

of bleach and one cup (250ml) of detergent mixed in three gallons (12l) of water (while even a strong bleach solution won't change the color of the fabric, bleach residues can be damaging to clothing). To be fully weatherproof, any kind of outdoor cushions must be filled with a water-shedding polyester fiberfill; it is important that water be able to flow easily through the cushion.

EXTRA COMFORTS

Every good beach house needs a place by the door where straw hats, flip-flops, and dip nets can be stored. Here we pause to brush off the sand and drop our beach things, a slight interruption in the flow from outdoors to in.

An outdoor shower floored with pressure-treated lumber is a small but welcome luxury (make sure the boards underfoot are widely spaced so that water drains easily). The soft sluice of fresh water rinsing away dried salt and sand feels wonderful after the sting of waves. Warm water is not a necessity, but it is certainly appreciated—there's something glorious about showering in hot water under the open sky on a cool morning or in the chill of early evening.

A cabinet or row of hooks keeps fresh towels within reach, and a clothesline nearby is handy for hanging wet bathing suits. With plumbing already in place, it is easy to install an outdoor sink

A small outdoor shower is given the look of a classic garden structure, a creative way to make this amenity work with a fairly formal house.

Even when a full-scale shower facility isn't possible, a place to rinse off can be added almost anywhere. The nearby stairs provide a spot to set towels and flip-flops temporarily.

for cleaning fish and a low spigot near the bottom of the stairs for rinsing off sandy feet.

GARDENING AT THE WATER'S EDGE

While there seems to be a delicious paradox in delicate blooms surviving in the presence of the earth's most awesome elements, a seaside garden can grow and thrive if it is planted with hardy, wind-tolerant species.

Flowers for Every Garden

The plants that perform best are those native to the region, so keep an eye out for the flowers and foliage plants that prosper in your area, and consider them for your garden. Oxeye daisies, coneflowers, wild blue lupines, rugosa roses, and Cape Cod's famous rambling roses grow well in the North; cosmos, sweet William, alyssum, and crimson clover thrive in the South; sand beans, beach sunflowers, and portulaca flourish along the Gulf Coast; flax and Indian blanket

Even with the sand and the salt, a garden can flourish by the sea. Here, a bed filled with a rainbow of dahlias defines the lawn with blazing color.

The blooms of a pale purple hydrangea
evoke the days of high summer. These
shrubs have been set close to the house,
so that they are somewhat sheltered

from the winds, and their owners
take care to give them the water and
fertilizer they need.

feel at home in Southern California; and beach asters, marguerites,
and wild snapdragons, abound in the Pacific Northwest.

Choosing a good location is especially important, because
a garden at the ocean needs not only abundant sunshine and mois-
ture, but also shelter from the wind. If your garden site is exposed
to the wind, you might create a windbreak to protect the plants. A
fence, a tall hedge of wind-tolerant shrubs, or a berm—a mound or
bank of earth—can all help shield plants from the wind.

Even if you have no proper garden space, you can create
a miniature garden of potted plants and hanging baskets. The
virtue of container gardening is that you can alter the soil mix and
control the amount of sun the plant receives, allowing you to grow
specimens that would otherwise be unavailable to you. And pretty
terra-cotta or ceramic pots filled to overflow with cheerful geraniums or easy-care petunias will also ornament your porch or deck,
rendering it a garden above the ground.

A combination of foliage and flowers will create an ever-
changing backdrop for the garden, whether you are planting in the
ground or in containers. Plan flower plantings around the seasons
by blending annuals and perennials that take the garden from early
spring through autumn. For texture and continuity, pair showy
specimens with ornamental foliage plants or flowering shrubs that

remain attractive after blooming. To keep the feeling natural, native plants can be generously interspersed with cultivated varieties. An easy-care groundcover forms a beautiful canvas for any sort of garden, adding color and texture all year long.

Whether you opt for a wildflower meadow or a carefully cultivated garden, plantings can soften the transition down the slope from house to shore, unfolding in a sequence of garden vignettes that makes you feel as though you are passing through a series of rooms. Connect these "rooms" by establishing a meandering path edged with stone. Stones dug up as the soil is prepared can be used for retaining walls, fences, and other borders.

Decorating the Garden

Garden ornaments can help to define special places and direct the eye—even a single urn in a small corner can have a big impact when filled with hot pink flowers and ivy trailing down the side. For gardening budgets that don't stretch far enough to include antique urns and statuary, modern technology offers several alternatives. Some manufacturers produce ornaments of "cast stone," a material first used by the resourceful Victorians as an inexpensive substitute for carved stone. Similar in principle to concrete, cast stone is made up of marble or other stone dust that can be cast in

a mold and finished to look very much like the real thing. And like the carved variety, cast stone takes on the patina of age as the years pass, although it is somewhat more fragile.

Even newer are pieces cast from a mixture of fiberglass-like resin and stone dust that can be colored to look like anything from terra-cotta to lead. While unresponsive to the gentle aging processes that stone and metal undergo, such furnishings can be startlingly accurate in detail. Resin reproductions have become popular lately, not only because of their reasonable price, but also for their light weight and sturdiness.

Particularly in a shore garden, where square footage is often precious, garden structures can both expand a garden's usable space and frame a view. Even something as small as a garden bench is a welcome amenity in a seaside garden. Much more than just a place to sit, a bench is an invitation to contemplate one's surroundings. It can also function as a focal point—a design element that is almost as restful to look at as it is to sit on, whether it is turned toward the ocean view or tucked into a sheltered corner of the garden. Garden benches can be constructed of a variety of materials, from durable teak—which over time weathers to a soft gray—to rustic branches to stone stained with soft patches of green and blue lichen (a sign of a healthy environment: lichen is sensitive to air pollution).

Lush tropical plants complement this
open-air pavilion, which is bordered
by a pretty bi-level pool.

A bench can be as simple as a plank resting on two tree stumps or as elaborate as a Victorian confection in wrought iron. Iron is susceptible to salt air, but vintage metal furniture has a charm that may make the extra maintenance worth it. To keep iron furniture in good shape, scrape rust spots with a stiff wire brush, then clean thoroughly with turpentine, prime with a primer designed for metal, and finish with exterior semigloss or gloss enamel.

Trellises and fences can help create a sense of separate spaces, each one shady and private. Well-placed garden structures can also draw the eye toward a garden's best features, creating a pleasant view for every season. At the same time, they disguise the less-than-attractive ones. A handsome fence, for instance, conceals trash cans from view, while providing support for flowering vines. A stone retaining wall can be planted with sun-loving rock garden plants.

The rewards for maintaining a garden can be enjoyed every day in bouquets of flowers, greenery, and aromatic herbs. Almost anything that will hold water can be turned into a vase: a preserves jar, an old enamelware coffee pot, a vintage milk bottle found washed up on shore. As the summer progresses, the bouquets change, marking the passing of another season by the sea, until at summer's end, heralded by asters and goldenrods, the chill morning air leaves a rim of frost on each blade of golden grass.

A POSTSCRIPT

A house by the sea is "home" whittled down to its essence, and life there is likewise simplified. The wind blows away our inland habits, and we shed not just city clothes but city gadgets, city schedules, and city distractions. We find ourselves inexpressibly thankful for a dress code of bathing suit, sandals, and sunscreen. We live for the deliciously simple routine: walk in the early morning, read after breakfast, sail or swim at midday, cook in the afternoon. After a day, a weekend, a summer of blissful contentment, we are sustained through the winter by thoughts of moments past and of those yet to be lived in our homes by the sea.

A rowboat painted in honor of the sea and sky is poised for an afternoon fishing expedition in the salty bay.

SOURCES

Anthropologie
(800) 309-2500
Stores Nationwide
Lanterns and indoor and outdoor furnishings

Brown Jordan
9860 Gidley Street
El Monte, CA 91731
(818) 443-8971
Outdoor furniture

Casablanca Fan Company
761 Corporate Center Drive
Pomona, CA 91768
(888) 227-2178
Ceiling fans

Crate & Barrel
725 Landwehr Road
Northbrook, IL 60065
(800) 606-6387
Call for store locations
Indoor and outdoor furniture and accessories

Fran's Wicker and Rattan Furniture
295 Route 10
Succasunna, NJ 07876
(800) 531-1511
Wicker and rattan furniture

Giati Designs, Inc.
614 Santa Barbara Street
Santa Barbara, CA 93101
(805) 965-6535
Teak furniture, sun umbrellas, and exterior textiles

Lloyd Flanders
3010 10th Street
P.O. Box 550
Menominee, MI 49858
(906) 863-4491
All-weather wicker furniture

Old Hickory Furniture Company
403 S. Noble Street
Shelbyville IN 46176
(800) 232-2275
Rustic furniture

Smith & Hawken
117 East Strawberry Drive
Mill Valley, CA 94941
(800) 776-3336
Garden furniture and other items via mail order

Pier 1 Imports
301 Commerce Street
Suite 600
Fort Worth, TX 76102
(800) 245-4595
Furnishings and Accessories

Vintage Wood Works
Highway 34 South
Quinlan, TX 75474
(903) 356-2158
Wooden doors and decorative trim

Winston Furniture Company
160 Village Street
Birmingham, Al 35124
(205) 980-4333
Casual furniture

ADVICE

American Institute of Architects
1736 New York Ave. NW
Washington, DC 20006
(202) 546-3480

American Society of Interior Designers
608 Massachusetts Ave. NE
Washington, DC 20002
(202) 646-3480

National Association of the Remodeling Industries
4301 Fairfax Drive
Suite 310
Arlington, VA 22203
(703) 276-7600

National Paint & Coatings Association
1500 Rhode Island Ave. NW
Washington, DC 20005
(202) 562-6272

CANADA

Chateau D'Aujourd'Hui
6375 Rue Saint Hubert
Montreal, Quebec
(514) 228-4191

Quintessence Designs
1222 Young Street
Toronto, Ontario
(416) 921-3040

Ziggurat
254 King Street East
Toronto, Ontario
(416) 362-5900

INDEX

PHOTO CREDITS